Canadian History Stories

50 True and Fascinating Tales of Major Events and People from Canada's Past

Table of Contents

Introduction

Officially founded in 1867 (but with foundations laid much earlier), Canada is a land of opulent natural resources, unfathomable distances, and an even richer history. With historical ties to the United Kingdom and France, grappling with the country's bygones undoubtedly promises to be a fascinating tale. While traditionally supporting both sides during international conflicts, Canada has seen social and political changes, uneasy relationships between its various parts, evolutions in its cultural relationships and education, and more. This book will introduce you to the vast domain of Canadian history and cover an engaging selection of information presented through recounting riveting historical events.

You'll learn about the impact of the French and early British colonization and how these were seen from the perspective of the Indigenous people. Through the stories of the trials and tribulations affecting these nations, you'll learn about their role in shaping modern Canadian society. These stories depict the coming together of many different cultures – a process that was neither short nor smooth. Still, how it came to be holds valuable lessons about conflicts and resolutions – just as the stories of wars and times of hardships do. The evolution of the Canadian government took an interesting path, beginning with its formation and initial stages of state-building, continuing with a prolonged maturation period, developing regional differences, and the eventual blossoming of the prim ordinary colonies into the provinces we know today.

One chapter is dedicated to the Confederation, while several others detail the many elements of nation-building, like wars and other twists and turns of Canada's historical tapestry. Unlike other books in its category, this one also provides an in-depth insight into the socio-economic fluctuations, regional contrasts, and the development of cultural identities that followed these events.

Whether you're a history aficionado looking to learn more about Canadian history or a novice in the field, you'll find answers to some of the most burning questions regarding the country's past in a cohesive, comprehensive, yet easy-to-digest packaging. If you're interested in learning what life in Canada looked like at the time it consisted of a few British colonies or under the rule of the French Empire, or wish to study its history from an Indigenous culture point of view, you won't be disappointed. As you'll soon learn, Canada, like many other countries, grew through continuous changes while retaining some of its core traditions. If you're interested in partaking in a voyage that shows how a small patch of land from the 15th century went through a tumultuous evolution to re-emerge as a populous and inclusive environment where different nations coexist nowadays, please keep reading!

Chapter 1: Indigenous Stories

Beginning with the tale of Turtle Island, this chapter will introduce you to the world and culture of the Indigenous people of Canada. Next, you'll learn about the Inuit and Métis peoples' ancestral roots, cultural traditions, and spiritual beliefs, starting with a story of how the Inuits managed to survive and thrive in the harsh conditions ruling their homeland. Moving on, you'll read about the Métis peoples' concerns regarding their lands. The story of the Great Whale Project illustrates the Inuit peoples' exceptional adaptation methods to Canada's challenging environments. In the last story, you'll read about the modern repercussions of historical events on these communities as they try to embrace their past to reclaim their future.

1. Turtle Island: The Beginning of Time

Before there were people, there was a flooded world – the earth cleansed of fighting and greed. All that was left were some animals surviving in the water, notably the loons, muskrats, and turtles. All was quiet and peaceful, and new life was waiting to rise in the calm of the slowly moving ocean.

Nanabush, a supernatural being with the power to create new life, tasked the animals with finding soil. The turtle tried first but could not find soil beneath the waves in the darkness. The loon tried, but its wings could only take it so far before it had to come back up for air. The muskrat, the last hope, dove deep. It was gone for a long time, given up for dead, but eventually rose above the water, holding a clump of earth.

The turtle tried to find soil beneath the waves after being tasked by the Nanabush.

Nanabush took the soil and placed it on the turtle's back. The small floating island of soil became North America, and life was created again.

Many cultures tell a story of a great flood that cleaned the world before life was created anew. Turtle Island's story is told by many indigenous cultures across Canada – the oral traditions have been passed down over thousands of years. Nanabush is known as Nanabozo in some stories or Weesakayjack in others. Other stories, such as Sky Woman, tell of the heavens where supernatural beings live.

Sky Woman fell through a hole in the heavens and descended toward the earth, guided by the birds. She fell onto the back of a turtle and was saved. In some stories, she is thankful and uses her power to grow soil around her, creating Turtle Island. In others, the animals dove to the bottom of the ocean to retrieve the soil. The people who populated the land are Sky Woman's descendants.

The Indigenous culture in Canada is as rich as the soil that birthed the nation. The indigenous people can be traced back thousands of years, well before the time of the settlers, and they were as diverse as the world is today. The oral stories handed down from generation to generation share similar themes but differ in the details. Those differences might be slight or significant.

The story of Turtle Island is a call to action. It is one or many stories, depending on how it is viewed, but it is still only one story of many. To truly understand the Indigenous people of Canada, their stories must be researched and read. Just as the soil was brought from the bottom of the ocean, history must be brought to the surface to understand what Canada is as a nation.

2. Arctic Adaptation: Survival and Societies of the Inuit

In the far Northern reaches of Canada lies a barren landscape of white. Life for the Inuit when they came to Canada 4,000 years ago from Siberia and beyond was both permanent and temporary.

It was permanent because they knew how to thrive in such conditions. They could hunt polar bears, arctic foxes, fish, and seals with only sharpened spears and rudimentary fishing equipment, and they could outlast the bitter cold that threatened to take lives every year. They passed down knowledge from elders to children to preserve it for millennia.

And it was temporary. Many First Nations societies were nomadic, moving from one place to another with what they needed to find the food and tools to survive another year. They built igloos in the winter and ice houses in the summer. And once the ice had melted and the Inuit people had moved on, the land returned to a blank ice sheet once more.

This way of life sounds far removed from modern-day society. Yet, there is much more in common with life in the Canadian tundra 4,000 years ago than first meets the eye. Inuit parents did not give their children physical punishment, talking with them instead. Children were often named after revered and respected family members, and there was a dedicated focus on education.

In many ways, people could benefit from revisiting the ways of the Canadian Inuit when life was simpler; people lived in communities, helping each other and caring little for physical possessions (they only carried what they needed or helped them to survive).

Modern society cannot return to these simpler times, and neither will the Inuit. Over time, they have adapted to be less nomadic, and instead of the simple igloos they once lived in, they now live in permanent houses equipped with power. They have lived in an autonomous territory, Nunavut, since 1999. They use modern tools and methods but still hunt and fish as they did thousands of years ago, and the knowledge is still passed down from elder to child.

And still, modern society can learn a thing or two from the Inuit. The natural world is a finely balanced ecosystem, and if too much is taken, it will fail. The Inuit people hunt and fish for food, clothes, and tools. They take from oceans, rivers, and land but don't take too much. They have over 4,000 years of history and knowledge and understand how the natural environment can be destroyed. The Inuit might have adopted modern techniques only because they have become available. How many nations around the world could have all modern technology taken from them and be able to survive in their climate?

The answer would be very few.

Of those who could survive, the Inuit would be smack-dab in the middle. They have been a part of Canada from a time before Canada was Canada, and if history tells us anything, it's that they will outlive many. And while it is never a good thing to think about the disappearance of nations and people, removing the trapping of modern society from Inuit culture might not be a bad thing.

Along with the adoption of modern society came the curses, epidemics like alcoholism, disease, and even higher death rates.

The changes have been extremely challenging for many Indigenous cultures across Canada, and there are no easy answers to life's current problems. All that can be clung to is resilience and endurance. The Inuit people, like all Indigenous peoples across Canada, are nothing if not resilient. They have lived through extreme conditions and hardships, and time will tell how they adapt to the world's current challenges.

3. Louis Riel and the Red River Rebellion: A Métis Uprising

Louis Riel.
https://commons.wikimedia.org/wiki/File:Louis_Riel.jpg

After its foundation in 1867, Canada acquired new territories, including the territory of Rupert's Land – the land governed by Rupert, King Charles II's cousin, who bestowed it to the Hudson's Bay Company. This fertile land was at the drainage basin of Hudson Bay, East Canada's largest sea indenting. There was only one problem. The territory was populated by the Red River Colony, who took offense when the old administration transferred their homeland to Canada without consultation, much less consent.

The founders of the Red River Colony were Scottish settlers who had arrived at the confluence of the Assiniboine and Red River of the North around 1812. In 1836, the Hudson's Bay Company took over the settlement's administration, now inhabited by the descendants of English and French trappers and travelers lured to the West by the fur trade. Born from mixed European and Native American unions were the Métis people, who were not at all content with their regime – and for a good reason. During the Hudson's Bay administration, they lost a lot. It started with their trading privileges, which had made their country thrive in the first place. And, of course, there was the lack of protection from constant threats from all sides. The United States, Canada, and Britain were all after Hudson's Bay's territories, and Canada managed to monopolize those in the North West.

At this, the Métis were greatly concerned about losing even more, including their land rights and cultural heritage. Their fears weren't unfounded. Even before their territory was officially transferred to Canada, Protestant settlers appeared in the colony and started propagating their religion and culture – in an attempt to push back the Métis. Once again, the Red River Colony had no help defending themselves against this intrusive behavior. The negotiations for transferring the land went ahead as if it were a barren territory without human inhabitants.

To make matters worse, the Canadian government attempted to re-survey the Métis farms stretching alongside the local rivers. Unfortunately, the Métis couldn't show clear titles to their land, and they were afraid that the regional government would not respect their occupancy rights. In other words, the Métis were in serious danger of losing their farms. In the middle of this chaos, one man stepped forward to act as a spokesman for the Red River Colony. His name was Louis Riel, and he was the leader of one of the Miss militant groups – the one that had prevented surveyors from entering the colony, sparking one of the most famous rebellions in Canadian history. The group led by Riel soon had the support of both English and French-speaking Métis communities. Since the Canadian government couldn't assume control at the pre-arranged time, the rebels took advantage of this hiatus. They held The Hudson's Bay Company's main trading post hostage until the Canadian government agreed to bargain with them. The rebels founded a provisional government, appointing Riel as its ruler. Their goal was to negotiate their entrance into the Canadian Confederation. Naturally, it didn't go smoothly, as armed conflicts were an everyday occurrence and even resulted in the death of Thomas Scott, a prisoner against Riel's provisional government.

After a chaotic winter made even colder by the frustration-filled negotiations, the Canadian government finally recognized the Red River Colony government and granted rights to its people. Still, the Metis victory was bittersweet. From then on, they had their own province (known as Manitoba,) a tiny territory compared to the vast land surrounding it, all of which belonged to the Canadian government. Even within Manitoba, the Métis only had control over their farms, and all public lands were still under Canadian governance. Even sadder, the land titles Canada initially guaranteed to reserve land for the future generation of the Métis were somehow lost along the way. Yet, the Métis people survived this and many other hardships and still thrive in Canada today.

4. The Great Whale Project: An Environmental Victory for the Inuit

The Great Whale River, with its magnificent sights of lichen-covered banks and forest-protected surroundings, empties into the Eastern side of Hudson Bay. It's the home of caribou herds and migratory birds traveling across following their seasonal patterns. In this subarctic paradise, Hydro-Quebec, a utility company, proposed to build a hydroelectric power system of never-before-seen proportions. With the first phase of the undertaking, known as James Projects, completed by 1990, they made plans to proceed to the second one, which entailed damming the river and erecting dikes to harness the river's kinetic energy. Known as the Great Whale project, the plans for the system promised not to resolve not only Quebec's mounting energy shortage issues but also those of neighboring New York.

However, where the leaders of Hydro-Quebec only saw the potential for generating millions of megawatts of energy, the locals saw a completely different picture. The indigenous communities living in the territory supplied by the Great Whale River feared that the project would disrupt the natural ecosystem, which has proven true. Even before the plans for the Great Whale project were fully formed, the first phase had already caused the death of 10,000 migratory caribou when another river was diverted. According to the environmentalists, the new project would likely cause alterations of the subarctic region in proportions rivaling rainforest destructions.

While Hydro-Quebec tried to assuage the fears of Indigenous peoples, promising to take care of the animals while the system was being built, they disregarded the fact that producing and transporting energy from the dams would cause further environmental pollution. And the Indigenous people, like the Inuit, knew how much harm this would cause their communities.

In 1984, during the works that preceded the Great Whale Project, toxic methylmercury leached into the LaGrande River. It was absorbed by the fish and the vegetation, rendering them unusable. And if the new project went ahead, the poison would also reach the Great Whale River. When the Indigenous communities raised concern about this (given that mercury causes birth defects, miscarriage, and stillbirths), they were told to avoid eating fish until the mercury levels subside. However, they would have to wait 25-30 years for this to happen. For the Inuit living in harsh and remorseless conditions, racked by wind and other natural forces, fish is the primary source of sustenance, especially during winter. Telling them not to eat fish is like telling them not to breathe.

The 6000 Inuit living in the region in question had enough of their worries being hushed. While the Canadian government promised to grant them power to nearly two-thirds of the Northwest Territories, they knew they wouldn't be dealt with fairly when it came to their fight against Hydro Quebec. After joining forces with the Crees, who also lived at the mouth of the Great Whale River, they hired experts to dismantle the claims that the project didn't threaten the destruction of the ecosystem in and around the river. They also started legal actions against Hydro Quebec and the Canadian government. Later, they took their dispute to the United States. In 1990, they traveled to New York in a sturdy Inuit kayak reinforced with the bow of an Indian canoe, protesting against the local energy companies buying energy from Hydro Quebec. Slowly but surely, their efforts started to pay off because, in 1994, both the New York Power Authority and Consolidated Edison (the primary buyers) canceled their contract with Hydro Quebec. Eventually, even the Canadian government got tired of the fight, putting the project on hold. The Inuit have won and could rest safely in the knowledge they saved their homeland – at least for now.

5. The History of Inuit and Métis: Knowing the Past to Claim the Future

The Inuit and the Métis people suffered innumerable losses throughout Canadian history. Disbanding their governments, banning traditional practices, and their language brought on by colonization were bound to have repercussions for their future. It denied them the chance to grow in their identities as other cultures are free to do. Now, their identity is tainted with the knowledge that they had to deny their own culture for what seemed like an eternity to survive. They couldn't celebrate their holidays because they were trying to blend in with a culture that overruled their own. And those who didn't assimilate suffered even more. The oppression of the Inuit and Métis people has had an enormous impact. The memories of the colonization period were passed down through the generations, and the descendants living in today's Canada still speak about those dark days. They can now speak freely about their despair while hiding their cultural identity – something they couldn't do for the longest time. However, it doesn't mean that they'll ever forget.

Other members of the younger generation remember being confused about their identity because their grandparents were still afraid to talk about their background. They were shamed for being who they were and wanted to spare the youth from the same fate. The middle generation also dealt with poverty and racism as a result of colonization. Together with the experience their parents told them was traumatic, to say the least.

The experiences of oppression definitely influenced the shaping of their self-identity. Some even walk with their head down to this day, fearing to draw attention to themselves. In the age of purported cultural diversity and acceptance, this might be surprising to many – but it is the reality of the Inuit and Métis people.

Some learned about their heritage only recently, as their grandparents and great-grandparents never embraced their Indigenous roots. They claimed to be either English or French, so that's what their descendants grew up believing themselves to be. It took the generation that had access to technology to educate themselves to learn the truth and understand why it was hidden from them. Others lament the loss of their language as a result of colonization.

Despite these experiences, the Inuit and the Métis now look forward to reclaiming and strengthening their identity. While the generation feels more empowered to begin this journey, the older generations are also becoming open to embracing their roots. They might never be able to proclaim their identity proudly as an Inuit or Métis. Still, they at least acknowledge who they are and where they came from.

What young and old generations agree on is that their future will be forever connected to their past. They know how challenging it is to break the cycle of shame and hiding and how much resilience it takes. Some speak about the mental health issues caused by their family's intergenerational trauma brought on by colonization. For the Métis people, this pain was further aggravated by the impacts of residential and day schools. Children were removed from their communities for generations, cutting them off from a normal cultural childhood. It also made the children's parents ashamed that they couldn't give their children what they had received in the residential schools. When children who went to these schools grew up and had children of their own, they were at a loss of how to raise them, having not had the guidance of the strict regime they were raised by.

Discussions about their connection to their land also bring up bittersweet memories for the Inuit and the Métis communities. For the longest time, they had responsibilities but no rights to their lands, which made passing on their culture even harder. These communities thrived because they knew nature and felt a connection to their land. Without this connection, they felt untethered and at a loss to teach the next generations how to grow by working hard with nature.

Despite the many challenges they faced due to colonialism, the Inuit and the Métis people of today's Canada are breaking their silence. They feel lucky to know where they come from, ready to embrace the inner strength and courage that allowed their past generations to survive hardships and injustices.

Chapter 2: Stories of Jacques Cartier

The story of how Christopher Columbus sailed to the New World of the Americas, reaching the Caribbean in 1492, is fairly well known. The much lesser-known expedition of Jacques Cartier, the intrepid French explorer who not only ventured where few had dared to go but also claimed a vast land for the lilies of France, invites you to set sail once more into the hazy depths of history. While Columbus's exploits have taken center stage in the annals of exploration, Cartier's journey would soon reveal a treasure trove of its own – a tale of uncharted territories, royal intrigue, and a quest that would ultimately imprint the French fleur-de-lis upon the rugged, untamed landscape of Canada.

Jacques Cartier, the intrepid French explorer.
https://commons.wikimedia.org/wiki/File:Jacques_Cartier_1851-1852.jpg

6. Who Was Jacques Cartier?

Jacques Cartier was born around December 31, 1491, in the coastal town of Saint-Malo, Brittany, France. His birthplace, Saint-Malo, was renowned for its maritime traditions and served as the perfect backdrop for a young boy destined for a life at sea. From an early age, Cartier was surrounded by the ever-present seafaring culture in Saint-Malo. The salty breeze, the rhythmic cadence of ships in the harbor, and the stories of daring mariners returning from distant lands all worked together to shape his destiny. Born into a family of mariners, Cartier's upbringing was steeped in the lore of the ocean, and he quickly developed a fascination for the world beyond the horizon.

Cartier's natural inclination toward the sea became more prominent as he matured. He entered an apprenticeship with his uncles (ship owners in Saint-Malo) to further his maritime education. Under their mentorship, young Jacques received a comprehensive education in navigation, the art of seamanship, and the business of maritime trade. This apprenticeship was a crucial phase in Cartier's life. It equipped him with the practical skills required for a life at sea and exposed him to the broader world of exploration and trade. Saint-Malo, as a bustling port town, was a hub of activity and a melting pot of ideas, making it an ideal environment for a young man eager to learn and grow.

Cartier embarked on fishing expeditions in the North Atlantic as he honed his skills and knowledge. These early forays into the unpredictable and sometimes perilous waters of the Atlantic Ocean gave him the experience he needed to familiarize himself with the challenges of sailing and refine his navigational expertise. During these ventures, Cartier encountered the stark realities of life at sea, from the bitter cold of northern waters to the storms that tested the mettle of sailors. These experiences proved to be formative, providing him with the resilience and adaptability required for the difficult voyages ahead.

7. The European Push for Exploration

The dawn of the 16th century witnessed an era of unprecedented curiosity and ambition among European powers. The quest for new trade routes, the allure of exotic goods, and the drive to expand influence and wealth fueled a fervent desire for exploration. Jacques Cartier's historic journeys began within this backdrop of maritime competition.

In the early 16th century, Europe was in the throes of what would later be known as the Age of Exploration. The spice trade, which brought valuable goods from the East to Europe, had long been controlled by a network of middlemen, making spices and other exotic commodities exorbitantly expensive. European monarchs and merchants alike yearned to bypass these intermediaries and establish direct trade routes to the East, a quest driven by the promise of unimaginable wealth. This fervor for exploration was further fueled by the voyages of renowned explorers such as Christopher Columbus, who stumbled upon the Americas in 1492 while seeking a westward route to Asia. The discovery of these New World lands ignited the imaginations of European leaders, who now saw the potential for vast riches, new territories, and opportunities for missionary work in these uncharted realms.

In the midst of this atmosphere of exploration, Jacques Cartier embarked on his first historic voyage in 1534, setting sail from Saint-Malo, Brittany, under the patronage of King Francis I of France. Cartier's objective was to find a westward route to Asia, specifically a passage to the riches of the Orient, much like other explorers of his time. Cartier's expedition was equipped with two ships, the Grande Hermine and the Petite Hermine, manned by a crew of intrepid sailors and navigators. Their journey led them across the Atlantic Ocean to the eastern coast of North America, where they made landfall on the island of Newfoundland.

The significance of Cartier's arrival in Canada marked the beginning of his extensive exploration of the North American continent and his encounters with Indigenous peoples who inhabited these lands for millennia. Cartier ventured further inland during his first voyage, exploring the Gulf of St. Lawrence and areas along the coast of what is now Atlantic Canada. Along the way, he documented the region's geography, flora, and fauna, collecting invaluable knowledge of this uncharted territory.

While Cartier's first voyage did not yield the sought-after passage to Asia, it laid the groundwork for future exploration and solidified his reputation as a skilled navigator and explorer. His encounters with Indigenous people and documentation of the land would contribute significantly to the growing body of knowledge about the New World. In retrospect, Cartier's first voyage was more than a geographic discovery. It was the opening chapter in a narrative of exploration, cultural exchange, and the complex interactions that would shape the history of North America for centuries to come.

8. The Cross at Gaspe: The Symbol of a New Era

Jacques Cartier's voyages into the uncharted waters of the New World, particularly his three legendary expeditions between 1534 and 1543, were pivotal moments in history. Yet, within the narrative of Cartier's adventures, there is a lesser-known but profoundly symbolic episode that marks a turning point in his exploration – a moment that forever linked the Old World with the New, centered around the Cross at Gaspé.

The year was 1535, and Jacques Cartier was in the midst of his second voyage to the New World. His initial expedition in 1534 had brought him to the shores of Newfoundland, marking his first contact with North America. Now, Cartier was on a more ambitious quest that would take him deeper into the continent and the heart of what is now known as Canada. As he sailed along the eastern coast of North America, he reached a place of particular significance. This was Gaspé, a peninsula jutting out into the Gulf of Saint Lawrence. During his exploration of Gaspé, he and his crew stumbled upon an imposing sight – a towering, 30-foot-high wooden cross planted firmly into the ground. This cross, adorned with a shield bearing the fleur-de-lis – the emblem of France – stood as a silent sentinel, a marker left behind by earlier European explorers.

The cross at Gaspé was not an isolated find. It was part of a larger tradition among European explorers of claiming newly discovered lands on behalf of their respective countries and religions. In this case, the cross was a declaration of France's sovereignty over the territory and a symbol of the spread of Christianity to the New World. As customary during the Age of Exploration, Cartier wasted no time making his own mark on this new land. In a solemn ceremony, he took possession of the land and its inhabitants, proclaiming them subjects of King Francis I of France. Cartier planted a second cross next to the one he had discovered, a symbolic gesture signifying France's claim to the territory.

The act of taking possession, or "possession ceremony," was a recurring theme in European exploration during this era. It served to establish legal and territorial claims on behalf of the European powers, often accompanied by religious rites to assert Christianity's influence.

The Cross at Gaspé serves as a powerful symbol of the complex cultural encounters that unfolded during the Age of Exploration. It represented the collision of the Old and New World, European explorers and Indigenous peoples, religious beliefs, and traditions.

For the region's indigenous inhabitants, the arrival of Cartier and his men and the planting of the cross must have been a bewildering spectacle. The cross, a potent symbol of Christianity, was foreign to them, and the ceremonies accompanying its planting were equally unfamiliar. This encounter was a microcosm of the larger clash of cultures and beliefs that characterized the European exploration of the New World. It marked the beginning of a complex and often fraught relationship between the indigenous peoples of North America and the European colonizers.

9. First Contact: Cartier and the Iroquoian Encounter

In history, there are often moments when two worlds collide, and the reverberations of that encounter leave a permanent mark on the course of human development. One such moment occurred during Jacques Cartier's voyages to the New World in the early 16th century – an encounter that would forever alter the trajectory of North American exploration and the lives of the Indigenous people he encountered. This pivotal moment, often overlooked in favor of other chapters in Cartier's exploration, was his first contact with the Iroquoian peoples.

Jacques Cartier's second voyage, launched in 1535, had already yielded significant discoveries along the eastern coast of North America, including the discovery of the St. Lawrence River. At this point, Cartier was on a mission to explore the interior of the continent, believing that the river he had found might offer a passage to the riches of Asia. As Cartier sailed deeper into the heart of the continent, he and his crew soon reached a point that would resonate throughout history: their first encounter with the region's Indigenous people, specifically the Iroquoian-speaking St. Lawrence Iroquoians. The two groups were worlds apart, both culturally and technologically. The St. Lawrence Iroquoians were part of the rich tapestry of indigenous cultures that had thrived in North America for millennia, while Cartier's crew represented the vanguard of European exploration.

Language, of course, posed a formidable barrier to communication. Cartier and his crew could not converse directly with the St. Lawrence Iroquoians and vice versa. Nevertheless, the encounter was not without its exchanges. The Indigenous people offered furs and other goods, while Cartier reciprocated with European trinkets and gestures of goodwill. The initial interactions were characterized by mutual curiosity and a sense of wonder. For Cartier and his men, the St. Lawrence Iroquoians were living embodiments of the exotic and unknown, and the Indigenous people must have regarded the Europeans as beings from a distant and mysterious realm.

However, as the encounters continued, misunderstandings arose. Miscommunication, cultural differences, and the inevitable clash of worldviews led to tensions and conflict. These misunderstandings were not confined to Cartier's encounters. They were part and parcel of the broader pattern of contact between European explorers and indigenous peoples in the Americas. In conclusion, the first contact between Jacques Cartier and the St. Lawrence Iroquoians was a hugely influential moment in the history of exploration and colonization in North America. It was a meeting of worlds, a clash of cultures, and a turning point that would shape the continent's destiny.

10. The St. Lawrence River: The Route to New France

Jacques Cartier's voyages to the New World were marked by a relentless quest to discover a northwest passage to Asia, and his expeditions were not just about exploration but also strategic navigation. One of the most significant aspects of his journeys was his use of the St. Lawrence River as a crucial route to reach the heart of North America and establish the foundations of New France.

In 1534, during his first voyage, Cartier made landfall on the eastern coast of North America, specifically on the island of Newfoundland. While this voyage did not immediately lead him to the St. Lawrence River, it served as a stepping stone. Cartier was beginning to familiarize himself with the geography and the potential routes that could lead him further into the continent.

It was during his second voyage, in 1535, that Cartier encountered the mighty St. Lawrence River. Sailing up the river, he and his crew explored the waterway's depths, discovering the intricate network of tributaries and channels that would become central to their explorations. The St. Lawrence River became the main artery for Cartier's inland journey, offering access to the interior of North America as well as his first meeting with the St Lawrence Iroquoians.

Important discoveries punctuated Cartier's exploration of the St. Lawrence River. He reached a place he called "Mont Royal," the site of present-day Montreal, and continued upstream, ultimately reaching an Iroquoian village known as Hochelaga (modern-day Montreal). This journey revealed the river's potential for inland exploration and trade.

The St. Lawrence River was not merely a geographic feature but a strategic lifeline for Cartier's vision of New France.

Cartier's expeditions and use of the St. Lawrence River paved the way for future French exploration, trade, and settlement in North America. The establishment of Québec in 1608, at the confluence of the St. Lawrence and the St. Charles rivers, solidified France's presence in the region and marked the beginning of the enduring importance of the river to the colony of New France.

11. Effects of Cartier's Arrival on the Development of Canada

Jacques Cartier's arrival in what is now Canada had profound and multifaceted effects on the region's development. These positive and negative impacts reverberated through the centuries and played a pivotal role in shaping the history of Canada.

On the positive side, Cartier's voyages contributed significantly to European understanding of North America's geography. His maps and observations paved the way for future exploration and the eventual mapping of the continent. Cartier's interactions with indigenous peoples, notably the Mi'kmaq and St. Lawrence Iroquoians, initiated cultural exchanges and knowledge-sharing. These initial contacts introduced Europeans to the diversity of indigenous cultures and laid the foundation for future trade relationships. Finally, Cartier's voyages allowed France to claim territory in North America, which would become New France. This set the stage for further exploration and colonization by the French and the eventual development of Canada as a French colony.

On the other hand, the arrival of Europeans, including Cartier and his crew, introduced new diseases to indigenous populations, such as smallpox. These diseases had devastating effects, causing significant mortality. These early encounters foreshadowed the challenges and tensions that later characterized European-Indigenous relations.

Cartier's explorations set the stage for French colonization in Canada in the long run. The establishment of settlements, like Québec by Samuel de Champlain in 1608, and the development of the fur trade industry laid the foundations for New France. Over time, interactions between Europeans and Indigenous peoples led to cultural exchanges that enriched both societies. The fur trade, for example, encouraged cooperation and the exchange of goods and knowledge. The French heritage in Canada, rooted in Cartier's explorations, continues to influence Canadian culture, language, and institutions.

However, the competition for North American territory between European powers, particularly France and Britain, resulted in conflicts like the Seven Years' War. The Treaty of Paris in 1763, which ended the war, led to the cession of Canada to the British, marking the end of New France. As European colonization expanded, Indigenous people faced displacement and loss of their traditional lands. This process of dispossession had long-lasting consequences for these communities. European colonization disrupted traditional ways of life, as they were exposed to European customs, diseases, and technologies. This disruption contributed to cultural changes and challenges.

In conclusion, Jacques Cartier's arrival in Canada had far-reaching effects on the region's development, encompassing both positive contributions and negative consequences. His voyages initiated a complex web of interactions, exchanges, and conflicts that ultimately shaped the course of Canadian history, leaving a lasting legacy that continues to influence the nation's present-day identity and challenges.

Chapter 3: Stories of the Huron-Wendat and the Beaver Wars

To faithfully portray the infamous Beaver Wars, this chapter will introduce you to its most prominent cast members, the Huron-Wendat people. Besides detailing the nuances of their society, blossoming culture, and history, the chapter will also outline the strategic importance of fur during the era and how the clash over this commodity fueled conflicts with other Indigenous clans. In a tale about Sainte-Marie, you'll also learn how the French discovered Wendat's homeland. It showcases the dynamics of these wars, including the participants' (particularly the French and the Haudenosaunee) alliances and disastrous consequences. Through a harrowing tale of survival and loss, the chapter underscores the long-term effects these conflicts had on the Huron-Wendat, other tribes, and the formation of Canada. Lastly, you'll learn just how the European Intrusion into the Indigenous lives left the numbers of these hardworking tribes decimated.

12. The Blossoming of the Huron-Wendat Culture

The Huron-Wendat nation hailed from a branch of the Iroquoian people.
https://commons.wikimedia.org/wiki/File:Groupe_Huron-Wendat_Wendake_1880.jpg

The Huron-Wendat nation hailed from a northern branch of the Iroquoian peoples who, in the 17th century, populated the region bordered by Georgian Bay from one side and Lake Simcoe to the other. This area is known as Wendake by locals and Huronia by the French (Huron is a French word for Wendat). They formed a confederacy allying the nations of Ataronchronon (the Bog people), Tohontaenrat or Atahontaenrat (the Deer people), Attinniaoenten or Attignawantan (the Bear) people, Atingeennonniahak or Hatingeennonniahak (the Cord people), and the Arendarhonon (the Rock people). Their collective name, Wendat, means "island dwellers." While they spoke similar languages and had common roots, they operated under separate political ideologies. The Cord and Bear people were the first to populate the northern side of Lake Simcoe (located in modern-day Simcoe County, Ontario). They were joined by the three other nations who migrated from the northern side of Lake Ontario. Initially, the purpose of their alliance was to join forces temporarily against a common enemy, the Haudenosaunee nations, inhabiting the southern side of Lake Simcoe.

The term "Iroquoian" indicates an Indigenous linguistic family and traditional patterns, including Tuscarora (spoken along the mid-Atlantic coast), Cherokee (common in the southern Appalachians), and the Northern Iroquoians (inhabitants of the Great Lakes Region, where the Wendat people hail from). To make matters more confusing, the Europeans at the time started referring to the Haudenosaunee (Five Nations Confederacy) as "Iroquois," which sounded very similar to "Iroquoian."

Before they forged an alliance at Lake Simcoe, the Wendat ancestral communities lived along the rivers that emptied into Lake Ontario. After 300 years of living here, each nation had well-established and thriving villages, like Contarea, Ossossane, Teanaustaye, and Scanonaenrat, guarded by hundreds of armed fighters. By 1620, rumors of the Haudenosaunee attack reached these villages, and the Wendat prepared for the raiders. Except for the Deer people, the nations also had nearby settlements where they could take refuge during the harsh winters. Moreover, given their close economic ties with their northern neighbors, the Algonkian, the Wendat even permitted the Algonkian groups to spend the winter with them when the latter needed shelter. According to the 17th-century Jesuit records, the total Wendat population was estimated to be around 35,000 people. Their numbers peaked before 1634, just before the epidemics hit.

Through their expert knowledge of horticulture, the Wendats had built a thriving economy. They were particularly proud of the "three sisters" (squash, beans, and maize), which they supplemented with foraged plants, wild animals, and fish from the local rivers. They lived in houses covered in tree bark, built for extended families' on the maternal side (the Wendats traced their heritage through the female line in the family). As was customary among all the Iroquoian nations, the Huron Wendat's basic socio-economic community consisted of the matrilineal extended family, including all nuclear families, and women had a common point of origin through their grandmother or mother. The oldest common female relative of all women in the family was in charge of this entire small community. They all lived under the same roof, in a home varying in size depending on the size of the community. Wendats only had eight ancestral matrilineal lines. Everyone belonged to one of these common ancestors. It's also where the names the nations became known came from. Each ancestral community or clan had strict rules. For example, clan members couldn't marry each other. They could only marry outside their clans. Moreover, children could only marry members of their father's clan but not of their mothers. This is how clan memberships were extended beyond the village of the original families and into other locations. It allowed them to build a system where clans could rely on each other's help regardless of where and in which nation they lived. When the enemy or war threatened, everyone rallied to form an alliance.

Little by little, they integrated their villages within tribes, creating confederacies and a government with a shared structure, ceremonial practices, and belief systems. Two councils governed each village, one concerned with warfare. Whereas the other oversaw civil matters. There was no need for voting on who gets on the council. Men over the age of 30 automatically become members. However, not everyone had a voice in all matters. Elected chiefs from distinguished families and other elders decided on most issues due to their status and oratory prowess. The women had no voice in the council either.

13. The Rise and Fall of Sainte-Marie

Settling on the eastern shores of Georgian Bay, the Huron-Wendat nation found their ancestral homeland amid wooded hillsides and plenty of fertile land. The matrilineal society of exceptional traders thrived on this land they called the Wendake (which translates to "the land apart"). Their territory was first discovered by French explorer Samuel de Champlain, whose visit was soon followed by French Jesuit priests in the 17th century. Determined to spread the Christian faith wherever they went and believing that the best way to save the souls of those they encountered was to educate them, the Jesuits immediately started preaching to the Indigenous people.

While the missionaries took time to learn the Wendat customs and language, assimilating into their community, the Jesuit's superior, Father Jérome Lalemant, advocated for building a retreat for the priests. In 1639, they engaged French laborers to build a home away from the Wendat villages on the banks of the Isaraqui River. The Wendat-Hurons named it Sainte-Marie, and it soon grew into a self-sufficient missionary settlement. Besides the hardworking Frenchmen who helped build it, the mission was frequently visited by the priests and the Huron-Wendat people, too. The locals thrived on fur trading, fishing, and agriculture. The Story of Sainte-Marie was well known in France due to the regular reports the Jesuit superior made to French religious leaders.

These reports also explain why the Jesuits abandoned the mission only after a decade of its existence. By 1649, the Haudenosaunee Nation had attacked the Huron-Wendat communities numerous times, wearing down their defense. By this time, the Huron-Wendat were also decimated by epidemics. Their numbers were so low they couldn't even defend Wendake, much less Sainte-Marie. Seeing the looming threat and no possibility for backup, the Jesuits, the French workmen, and the newly converted Wendats abandoned the mission. Amid heartbreak and despair, they journeyed to St. Joseph Island, where they intended to establish a new base. However, after a cruel winter that left them starving and continued attacks from the Haudenosaunee, they abandoned their attempt, and everyone but the Jesuits fled to Quebec. The graves of the priests who refused to leave and died as martyrs became a place of pilgrimage.

14. A Clash for Commodities: The Initiation of the Beaver Wars

As their communities grew, the Huron-Wendat developed close social, trading, and political relationships with several nations alongside the Georgian Bay. Beans, corn, tobacco, cord made of Indian hemp, seashells, catlinite, copper, and many other commodities exchanged hands within these nations. Their military alliance, forged in 1609 against the common enemy, the Haudenosaunee, brought them even closer. However, the latter also consisted of strongly united nations (known as the Iroquois Confederacy by the Europeans). The Haudenosaunee were better organized than their adversaries, although they suffered a minor setback when the Europeans entered the scene and developed a taste for beaver pelts. The Indigenous people happily supplied it because they received muskets, powder, and balls through a mutually beneficial barter system. However, this only fueled conflicts between the tribes, leading to the beginning of the Beaver Wars. The tribe with the most furs would obtain the most ammunition and dominate the area.

Until the second half of the 17th century, the Haudenosaunee had plenty of beavers to hunt in their home region. However, as the beaver population became depleted, they were forced to look for their fur source in the territories of their adversaries. From 1677, the English aided their efforts.

In an attempt to take back dominion over the fur trade and push back the aggressive advancement of the Haudenosaunee, the Huron-Wendats aligned themselves with the French, who were more than happy to extend their assistance, given that they depended on the fur trade.

While the Haudenosaunees' attempt to dominate the fur trade was a strong enough conflict-inducing act in itself, the war was also heavily driven by French fur dependence. The French weren't picky about where and how the pelts got to their base in Montreal either. At one point, they even encouraged their ally tribes to hire warriors who didn't belong to their tribe (mostly belonging to the Algonquian nation) to help them deliver the fur. In retaliation, the Haudenosaunee attacked any tribes they discovered delivering fur to the French or their middlemen.

An era of hostile confrontations ensued, making the Beaver Wars one of the darkest periods in North American history. As the Haudenosaunee advanced toward the West, they reshaped tribal geography. This led to the destruction of numerous Indigenous confederacies, including the Huron-Wendats. Other nations only survived because they were fast to flee to the very border of the Mississippi River. The Beaver Wars also decimated Wendat's neighbors, the Algonquians, and others moved even farther to avoid further conflicts. At one point, over 20,000 refugees gathered in the small area of Wisconsin's Door Peninsula, which couldn't support an influx of these proportions. As a result, the tribes began to fight among themselves while trying to establish hunting territory – while others starved or fell victim to the several epidemics that spread through the area.

15. The Vanishing Huron-Wendat: A Tale of Survival and Loss

Once a thriving community of over 30,000 members, between 1634 and 1642, the Wendat's number dwindled down to 9,000. Most of them fell victim to a series of epidemics, including smallpox, measles, and influenza. Afterward, their ranks dwindled even more – only to have a little over 4,000 registered members by the 21st century.

At the height of their prime, the Wendats had 18-25 thriving villages of up to 3,500 inhabitants. During the warmer months, they supported their entire population with crops they grew and game they hunted on and off their lands. When the French arrived at Wendake in the early

17th century, the Wendats governed a massive territory, more than enough for their tribes to sustain their tribes. They had enough resources and manpower to fortify larger villages. These villages were strategically placed near a solid water supply and arable lands and built on a slight rise to avoid flooding as they were near the riverbank. However, they would deplete the firewood sources and soil nutrients every ten years or so, forcing them to move to more fertile territories.

Unfortunately, the Wendats could only go as far as they ran into enemy tribes searching for the same resources. By 1642, the Haudenosaunee reached the Ottawa Valley, defeated the Algonquians, and disbanded the Huron-Wendats. Following this time, the Wendats had further conflicts with other tribes, decimating their already scarce post-epidemic population.

During the Beaver Wars, some Wendats, like the Rock and the Deer people, saw salvation in joining the Haudenosaunee. The over 3,000 former Wendats, now fortifying the enemy's ranks, settled among the Onöndowa'ga (or Seneca). These were mostly followers of the old traditions, while 1,000 or so Christian Wendats followed the Jesuits to Georgian Bay.

After enduring a harsh winter and famine, the remaining 300 Wendats settled on Île d'Orléans. Another group of refugees later joined them. The settlement comprising the Bear, Cord, and Rock people now had a little over 600 members who wanted nothing more than to live peacefully and rebuild their community. However, fate had other plans. To ensure the continuation of their fur supply, the French made an agreement with the Haudenosaunee. According to this, all Wendats would join the ranks of Haudenosaunee, including the ones trying to settle further away. This is how those remaining 600 lost hope of maintaining their identity. They saw themselves disappear while assimilating with their enemies. Still, not all bowed down. Some of the Cord and Bear people fled to Lorette, where they still reside. Lorette is part of the territory that would later become Canada – more precisely, Manitoba, a province that played a crucial role in the history of Indigenous people and the rich evolution of the Canadian past.

A tiny fraction of traditional Wendats refused to join the Haudenosaunee and moved to the Tionontati in 1649. This community was later named the Wyandot (or Wyandotte in the United States), which some claim was an attempt to preserve their identity as Wendats. A couple of years later, they migrated near the Missii headwaters, where they clashed with the Dakota (Sioux), forcing them to move further to Chequamegon. At the beginning of the 18th century, the Wyandot, accompanied by the Odawa, settled on the outskirts of the newly founded city of Detroit. Three decades later, the Wyandot feuded with the Odawa and their French supporters, dividing their ranks into two. One migrated across from Detroit, while the other settled in the Ohio Valley. The former first aligned themselves with the French during the Seven Years' War and fought the English alongside the Pontiacs afterward. Their descendants live near Windsor (Ont), Canada.

On the other hand, the Ohio Valley group was forced to hand over their lands to the United States, which was only the beginning of their troubles. In 1830, The U.S. Congress published the Indian Removal Act, which allowed the government to relocate any Indigenous communities to reservations, which allowed them to move the Oklahoma Valley Wyandot to Kansas. In 1867, the remaining 200 members were moved again. This time, to an Oklahoma reservation.

16. European Intrusion: The Impact of the Fur Trade

At first, the trade the Wendats formed with the French explorers seemed like a good idea. It was lucrative on both sides, and the Europeans were on board with giving a helping hand against the Haudenosaunee. As a sign of solidarity with their Indigenous allies, French volunteers regularly joined the Wendats in their battles.

To fortify their military and create closer trade connections, the Wendats welcomed French missionaries with open arms, giving shelter and sustenance first to the Récollets in 1615 and then to the Jesuits in 1625. They were open to having them in their communities, although they knew where to draw the line. When asked to consider assimilation by matrimony, they refused several times. In their culture, a marriage was a partnership between two people and their extended families and had nothing to do with public matters. In other words, only the families could decide about weddings. The council had no say over the issue and couldn't arrange intermarriages with the French.

By the mid-1630s, the Wendats were France's largest pelt suppliers. They grew an extensive network of 500 men from several villages, who met suppliers en route to the French bases near St. Lawrence and exchanged the hides for French commodities. However, this well-oiled machine became seriously threatened when epidemics reduced the Wendats' numbers by half in just a few years, during the late 1630s and early 1640s. Although their neighbors, the Algonquian, suffered greater losses, the Wendats couldn't continue to supply fur at the same rate either. To keep up and remain on good terms with the French, they started looking for new territories, even though this put them in the path of the Haudenosaunee. Still, they were deeply committed to their French and hoped their allies would return the favor by providing military aid. While initially, the French seemed to be on their side, this soon changed.

The Haudenosaunee also suffered losses during the epidemics and had a rather twisted idea of replacing their members and regaining their strength. They saw the solution in warfare. They attacked the neighboring clans or fur trade rivals, killed their council members, and made the others join their ranks, allowing their families to survive. The Haudenosaunee warriors also relished the opportunity to absorb other powerful clans into one nation. Their plan worked because, by this time, they had the French on their side. Slowly but surely, the Wendat alliance coerced almost all Huron-Wendats to join the ranks of the Haudenosaunee. While they did this under the propaganda of forming one large, peaceful country, their actions greatly impacted Wendat identity. Once a well-represented member of the Iroquoian linguistic family, the Wendat language is now on the edge of extinction. After years of migrations to find better lands and living in shame after the Canadian colonization, the Wendats lost even more. Fortunately, there are several initiatives to revitalize their culture and language. Still, it will take many years to undo the damage caused by the past centuries, beginning with the faithful fur trade agreement.

Chapter 4: Tales of the Rise of French-Canadian Nationalism

The Huron-Wendat and the Beaver Wars were just the dramatic opening act for early Canada, as they set the stage for the epic tale of French-Canadian nationalism that was yet to unfold. Canadian land had been shuffled around like a deck of cards in a high-stakes poker game between empires. Having successfully established a rich culture in New France, the French found themselves at the center of territorial disputes, religious fervor, and the ever-elusive fur trade profits but emerged with a new sense of identity. The Huron-Wendat had shown them the way of resilience, and the Beaver Wars had revealed the value of strategic alliances. However, simmering under the seemingly peaceful surface were the issues of language, faith, and the unique blend of European and Indigenous influences that gave rise to the quintessential French-Canadian character.

17. The Battle of Quebec: Birth of Franco-Canadian Resilience

In the mid-18th century, the North American continent was a battleground of empires, where British and French colonial powers vied for supremacy. This narrative points to a pivotal moment in history – the Battle of Quebec in 1759, which shaped the course of French-Canadian identity. The roots of the Battle of Quebec trace back to a tangled web of colonial ambitions, territorial disputes, and centuries-old rivalries.

French explorers had long laid claim to vast territories in North America, while the British sought to expand their colonial holdings. By the mid-18th century, these ambitions collided in a clash of empires.

General Louis-Joseph de Montcalm.

The stage was set for confrontation, as the British under General James Wolfe and the French under General Louis-Joseph de Montcalm found themselves on opposing sides of the battlefield. Quebec, with its fortified walls, cliffs, and strategic location along the St. Lawrence River, became the epicenter of this struggle. On September 13, 1759, the two forces clashed outside the city walls of Quebec. The battle was brutal and costly, with both sides suffering heavy casualties. General Wolfe, leading a daring assault, managed to scale the cliffs and surprise the French defenders. Tragically, both commanding generals, Wolfe and Montcalm, were mortally wounded during the battle.

Ultimately, the British emerged victorious, and the French surrendered the city. This marked the beginning of British rule in Quebec and the subsequent transfer of New France to British control under the Treaty of Paris in 1763. The Battle of Quebec and the subsequent conquest of New France had far-reaching implications for the French-Canadian population. It was a moment that tested their resilience but also sowed the seeds of French-Canadian distinctiveness.

The French-Canadians, who had lived in New France for generations, faced the challenge of adapting to British rule. They were determined to preserve their cultural heritage and language, integral to their identity. The Catholic Church was central to French-Canadian society, providing a unifying force during and after the Conquest. The French-Canadians clung to their faith, further strengthening their cultural distinctiveness. Despite British dominance, French remained the language of everyday life. This linguistic resilience became a cornerstone of their identity. French-Canadians maintained strong ties to the land, often working as farmers in rural areas.

18. The Patriotes and the Rebellion of 1837: Seeds of French-Canadian Nationalism

Under British rule, French Canadians faced cultural and political challenges as the British imposed their legal and administrative systems, which often conflicted with the existing French-Canadian legal traditions. This created a sense of cultural alienation and discontent.

After the American Revolution, many English-speaking Loyalists migrated to British North America, further increasing the English-speaking population and accentuating their differences. French Canadians had limited political representation and influence within the colonial government, which English-speaking officials dominated. They had no say in the decisions that affected their lives.

In 1834, the Patriotes, led by figures like Louis-Joseph Papineau, Edmund Bailey O'Callaghan, and Louis-Joseph-Amable Trudeau, presented the 92 Resolutions to the British authorities in response to a series of grievances. These resolutions demanded significant constitutional reforms and greater political autonomy for Lower Canada (present-day Quebec). The Patriotes called for an elected legislative assembly to control taxation and government expenditures more. The 92 Resolutions emphasized the importance of protecting French-Canadian legal and civil rights, including the use of French in government proceedings.

The resolutions sought to limit the powers of the unelected legislative council and the governor, both seen as representing British interests rather than the French-Canadian majority. The presentation of the 92 Resolutions was met with resistance and opposition from the British authorities, who were reluctant to grant the requested reforms. This refusal naturally caused deeper resentment within the French-Canadian population.

Over time, a more radical faction within the Patriote movement began to gain influence. This group, led by individuals like Wolfred Nelson and Thomas Storrow Brown, grew frustrated with the slow progress of political reforms and began advocating for more direct and aggressive action. By 1837, tensions had reached a breaking point. The patriots, particularly in rural areas, began organizing armed resistance against the British authorities.

The Battle of Saint-Denis was one of the earliest confrontations of the rebellion. Under leaders like Wolfred Nelson and Jean-Olivier Chénier, patriot forces clashed with British troops. Although the Patriotes showed determination, they were ultimately outnumbered and outgunned, and the battle ended in defeat. Following the Battle of Saint-Denis, another skirmish took place in Saint-Charles, further illustrating the willingness of the patriots to engage in armed conflict to challenge British rule.

The British authorities declared martial law in Lower Canada in response to the rebellion. This move marked a significant escalation in the conflict. Martial law allowed for the widespread arrest of Patriotic leaders and supporters. Hundreds of individuals were taken into custody. Many Patriote leaders, including Louis-Joseph Papineau, fled to the United States to escape arrest. This significantly weakened the leadership of the Patriote movement.

The British authorities ultimately suppressed the rebellion, and the leaders faced harsh consequences. Louis-Joseph Papineau went into exile in the United States and later to France, where he lived until 1845. Thomas Storrow Brown was among those executed for their involvement in the rebellion. Others faced imprisonment, banishment, or other punitive measures.

While the rebellion was crushed, the events of 1837 left a lasting legacy. The struggle for political rights and representation continued, ultimately contributing to discussions around Confederation in the 1860s and the protection of French-Canadian culture and language within the

Canadian Federation. The willingness of the patriots to rise against British rule left a lasting legacy of defiance and resistance. This spirit of resistance would continue to influence the French-Canadian pursuit of political rights and representation.

While the rebellion was ultimately suppressed, it was a turning point in French-Canadian political activism. The events of 1837 galvanized the French-Canadian population to continue pushing for political reforms and representation. The Rebellion of 1837 laid the groundwork for discussions around confederation in the 1860s. French Canadians, recalling their earlier struggles for rights and representation, played a crucial role in shaping the terms of confederation to protect their heritage within the new Canadian federation.

19. The Aspirations of Henri Bourassa: A Voice for French-Canadian Nationalism

At the dawn of the 20th century, Canada was undergoing transformational shifts. The echoes of the confederation still resonated, and French-Canadians had secured certain protections and rights within the federation. However, a new era of change was underway. The shift from an agrarian to an industrial society was transforming the economic and social fabric of the country. Canada was becoming increasingly involved in international affairs, particularly through its ties to the British Empire.

Amidst these changes, Henri Bourassa emerged as a vocal advocate for French-Canadian nationalism. His contributions were multifaceted and deeply rooted in his personal convictions. Bourassa was unwavering in his commitment to preserving French-Canadian culture, language, and traditions. He believed that the survival of French-Canadian identity was essential and that assimilation into the English-speaking majority threatened the distinctiveness of his people.

One of the highlights of Bourassa's career was his fierce opposition to conscription during World War I. In 1917, as Canada's involvement in the war escalated, the government introduced conscription under Prime Minister Robert Borden to bolster the troops overseas. Bourassa vehemently opposed this measure because he believed that French Canadians should not be compelled to fight in a foreign war. He argued that the war was not a just cause for Canada and that conscription would be detrimental to French-Canadian interests.

In 1910, Henri Bourassa founded the newspaper Le Devoir, which became a powerful platform for his ideas and a prominent voice for French-Canadian nationalism. Bourassa championed the importance of protecting French-Canadian culture, language, and political rights through the newspaper. Bourassa believed in strong provincial autonomy as a means to protect French-Canadian interests. He saw this as a way to safeguard education, language, and culture within Quebec and other provinces with significant French-Canadian populations.

Henri Bourassa's ideas and writings influenced political thought in Quebec and across Canada. His arguments for linguistic and cultural preservation resonated with many French Canadians and impacted the broader discourse surrounding Canadian identity and nationalism.

20. The Quiet Revolution: Awakening of La Belle Province

In the turbulent 1960s, a seismic cultural and political shift began to reshape the province of Quebec. This transformation, known as the Quiet Revolution (Révolution tranquille), was a pivotal moment in the history of French-Canadian nationalism and the cultural identity of Quebec, often referred to as "La Belle Province" (The Beautiful Province).

The Quiet Revolution didn't emerge out of thin air. It was the result of decades of social, political, and economic developments that had laid the groundwork for change. Maurice Duplessis, Premier of Quebec from 1936 to 1939 and 1944 to 1959, was a conservative force in Quebec politics. A powerful Catholic Church, a stagnant economy, and a lack of social progress marked his era. This period was often called "La Grande Noirceur" (The Great Darkness). As the Premier of Quebec from 1960 to 1966, Lesage was the driving force behind many reforms that defined the Quiet Revolution. His Liberal Party of Quebec aimed to modernize the province, challenge the Church's dominance and promote secularism.

Quebec faced significant social and economic disparities, with rural areas lagging behind urban centers like Montreal. Many Quebecois lived in poverty, and the Catholic Church often controlled education. The long-standing historical themes were the desire for greater autonomy and the preservation of Quebecois culture and language. Events like the Asbestos Strike of 1949, which led to labor rights and demands for improved working conditions, served as precursors to the Quiet Revolution.

One of the first major moves of the Lesage government was the nationalization of hydroelectric power in Quebec. This decision gave the provincial government control over a valuable resource and a source of revenue. In a significant break from the past, the government asserted control over the education system, reducing the Church's influence. This secularization led to the creation of a modern, publicly funded education system.

Bill 101, passed in 1977, aimed to promote and protect the French language in Quebec. It mandated the use of French in the workplace, government, and education, and it remains a cornerstone of Quebec's language policy. The government introduced numerous social welfare programs, including a healthcare system, to address poverty and improve living conditions. These changes were a notable shift toward a more equitable society.

Quebec's cultural scene began to flourish during the Quiet Revolution. The province saw a surge in literature, film, and the arts. Figures like Leonard Cohen and Michel Tremblay emerged as popular icons.

21. The October Crisis: Nationalism at a Tipping Point

The roots of the October Crisis are traced back to the broader historical context of Quebec and Canada during the mid-20th century. The Quiet Revolution of the 1960s ushered in a period of profound change in Quebec. It challenged traditional norms, expanded the provincial government's role, and sought to assert Quebec's linguistic distinctiveness.

While the Quiet Revolution brought about positive changes in Quebec, it also gave rise to increased separatist sentiment. The Quiet Revolution had political consequences, including the emergence of the Parti Québécois (PQ) under René Lévesque. The PQ was founded on the principles of Quebec sovereignty, advocating for the province's independence from Canada.

Quebecois increasingly sought greater political autonomy within the Canadian federation. This desire was reflected in demands for constitutional changes and a more decentralized federation. The rise of the radical Front de libération du Québec (FLQ) added a violent element to the separatist movement. The FLQ, founded in the 1960s, was responsible for a series of bombings and kidnappings aimed at advancing their vision of an independent, socialist Quebec. Their actions heightened tensions and challenged the authorities' ability to maintain law and order.

The crisis began on October 5, 1970, when FLQ members kidnapped James Cross, the British Trade Commissioner to Canada, from his home in Montreal. The FLQ demanded the release of political prisoners and the publication of their manifesto. The emergence of the Front de libération du Québec (FLQ) played a crucial role in setting the stage for the October Crisis. The FLQ emerged as a radical separatist group influenced by Marxist-Leninist ideology. It aimed to establish an independent, socialist Quebec through violent means if necessary. The group's leaders believed such actions were necessary to advance their cause.

Leading up to the October Crisis, the FLQ carried out a series of bombings and acts of violence in Quebec. These included bombings at government buildings and targeted attacks on individuals associated with the government or the police. The FLQ's actions created a climate of fear and unrest in Quebec. The FLQ demanded the release of political prisoners, the publication of their manifesto, and the recognition of Quebec as an independent state. Their kidnappings and bombings were intended to pressure the authorities into meeting their demands and advancing their separatist agenda.

In response to the kidnapping, Prime Minister Trudeau invoked the War Measures Act on October 16, 1970, granting the federal government extraordinary powers, including military deployment, to maintain law and order. On October 10, 1970, the FLQ escalated its actions by kidnapping Pierre Laporte, a Quebec provincial cabinet minister. Tragically, Laporte was found dead on October 17, marking a devastating turn in the crisis. After 59 days in captivity, James Cross was released on December 3, 1970, in exchange for the safe passage of his kidnappers to Cuba. With the imposition of martial law, the Canadian authorities initiated a widespread crackdown on FLQ members and supporters. Many were arrested, and the organization was severely weakened.

In the short term, the crisis underscored the fragility of Canada's national unity. It revealed deep divisions and heightened tensions between Quebec and the rest of Canada. The government's invocation of the War Measures Act was controversial, leading to debates about the appropriate use of federal powers and civil liberties in times of crisis.

The crisis had political repercussions. Trudeau's handling of the situation earned both praise and criticism. Quebecers reelected the provincial government led by Premier Robert Bourassa, signaling their desire for stability and continuity. Under René Lévesque, the PQ distanced itself from the FLQ's violent methods. This distinction helped the party gain legitimacy and eventually win the 1976 Quebec provincial election.

In conclusion, the rise of French-Canadian nationalism represents a complex and enduring journey of cultural preservation, political struggle, and the pursuit of rights and recognition. One of the most significant contributions of French-Canadian nationalism has been preserving and celebrating the French language and culture in Canada. The enduring commitment to linguistic and cultural distinctiveness has left an indelible mark on Canadian society. Today, Canada proudly recognizes both English and French as official languages, reflecting a commitment to bilingualism that emerged from the struggles and aspirations of French Canadians.

From the Rebellion of 1837 to the Quiet Revolution and the October Crisis, these noteworthy events have shaped Canada's federal system and the delicate balance between provincial and federal powers. The evolution of French-Canadian nationalism offers valuable insights for other pluralistic and multilingual nations grappling with issues of identity and representation. Canada's commitment to protecting minority rights, promoting linguistic diversity, and fostering inclusivity serves as a model for nations seeking to navigate the complexities of cultural and linguistic diversity while maintaining national cohesion.

In today's Canada, the legacy of French-Canadian nationalism is celebrated in various ways, from bilingualism in government services to cultural festivals that showcase the vibrancy of French-Canadian heritage. The narratives of resilience, the pursuit of rights, and the commitment to cultural preservation continue to inspire Canadians from all backgrounds.

In the 21st century, Canada stands as a nation proud of its diversity, where the values of inclusion, multiculturalism, and respect for linguistic and cultural differences are woven into the fabric of society.

Chapter 5: Canadian Confederation Stories

Although Canada is one of the largest countries in the world today, history has shown its eventful path to unity. Before 1867, Canada was divided into three regions: Nova Scotia, New Brunswick, and the Province of Canada, which were all under British control. Things changed when these territories decided to join forces and gain their independence from the British. The act was called the Canadian Confederation and marked the birth of Canada as you know it today.

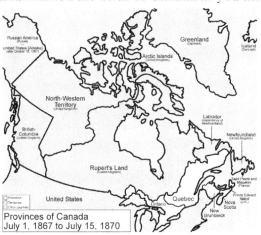

The Canadian provinces from 1867 to 1870.
No machine-readable author provided. Golbez assumed (based on copyright claims). CC BY-SA 3.0 <http://creativecommons.org/licenses/by-sa/3.0/>, via Wikimedia Commons: https://commons.wikimedia.org/wiki/File:Canada_provinces_1867-1870.png

So, what has prompted Canada to take this historic step? Many interesting events led to the Canadian Confederation, which will be discussed in this chapter.

22. Manifest Destiny

In the 1800s, the U.S. had big aspirations. This was obvious to Americans and non-Americans. Even their newspapers heavily discussed the topic. American journalist John Louis O'Sullivan coined the term "Manifest Destiny" when describing his country's ambitions. The term referred to the U.S. belief that it was destined to expand and take over North America. This started with acquiring Texas, but that wasn't enough. Its leaders and citizens urged the government to show the world their true power by taking over British territories, which included Nova Scotia, New Brunswick, and the Province of Canada.

At the time, the British Empire was expanding rapidly, and the Americans weren't comfortable with their presence in North America because they didn't trust them after the Revolutionary War. After the 1812 War, Britain was divided, which left it vulnerable and weak. This situation presented the perfect opportunity for America to take over the British colonies.

During the Civil War, the British were neutral and refused to take sides, or so it seemed. Behind the scenes, it was a whole different story. The British were privately helping the South to defeat the Northern states. The North was aware of the British's betrayal. Their newspaper called for expansion and taking control of Canada to make up for the lost colonies. On the other hand, the British wanted to take control of American territories in the north and the west to prevent the U.S. from annexing them.

Canada was aware of Manifest Destiny and America's ambition to expand. In 1867, America bought Alaska from Russia, leading Canada to worry they would be next. The provinces of Canada, New Brunswick, Nova Scotia, and other British colonies were shocked by the chaos and violence during the Civil War. They believed that the American government was weak and played a big role in the eruption of the war.

The colonies realized the only way to stand against America and free themselves from the British was by uniting and forming a strong government. They also could see that Britain wasn't willing to defend them in case of an American invasion.

The North ended up with an extremely powerful army after their victory in the Civil War. They were holding a grudge against the British for aiding the South against them and waiting for the opportunity to get revenge. A strong army and a weak enemy gave them the perfect opportunity to attack British colonies and achieve their goals.

Invading Canada was the only topic of discussion in the North. Their newspapers weren't discussing anything but the U.S. desire to annex Canada. Many political leaders in the country supported the invasion. The Canadians knew the North's threat was real, especially after purchasing Alaska.

The North started by canceling the free-trade deal with Britain and offering the three British colonies the chance to take Britain's place.

The political environment was shaky, and the British provinces feared the Northern invasion and were unwilling to pay for Britain's protection. They had to take action right away.

Confederation was the best option for the British and Canadians. It benefited Britain by allowing it to reduce its military and economic burden in America. If British colonies united and gained their independence from the U.K., Britain wouldn't be responsible for them. It was also an honorable way for Britain to walk away without experiencing shame or defeat. The British colonies also benefited from confederation as unity increased their strength and power.

Another reason for the Canadian Confederation was the difficulty of governing Canada East and Canada West under one legislature. Canada was flourishing and growing in every aspect, economically, politically, and socially. However, it was facing many issues. In Canada East, the English Catholic church was gaining so much power and was receiving a large amount of funds from the government.

In Canada West, English Protestants were weary of the French Catholic church. The constant tension between both countries resulted in political rifts and unstable governments. The situation got worse with the division between the Catholic and Protestant churches. The government struggled with trying to solve all of these problems. They needed to make certain changes that were currently impossible. They figured that joining the confederation could be their best solution.

Many countries were created from a war or a revolution. Blood, sweat, and tears were often spilled to gain their independence. However, this wasn't the case for Canada. The country was born out of negotiations and conferences.

23. Charlottetown Conference

The Charlottetown Conference was one of the most influential meetings of the Canadian Confederation and was the event that set the whole process in motion. The conference took place in September 1864 in Charlottetown, the capital of Prince Edward Island, and lasted for nine days. Representatives from Prince Edward Island, Nova Scotia, and New Brunswick organized the conference to discuss bringing the three territories together.

Interestingly, a group from the Province of Canada who weren't originally supposed to attend the conference played a huge role. They were the ones who convinced the rest of the provinces to sit and talk about their future and independence from Britain and the U.S.

This was no ordinary conference, as the parties didn't limit their discussions to politics. They spent their days feasting on luxurious meals, talking, and forming friendships. Perhaps this was a time for all the territories to realize they had more in common than they thought. On the eighth day of the conference, the organizers hosted a huge banquet, and the celebrations lasted all night. Afterward, it was back to business. After the conference, more meetings took place in Fredericton, Saint John, and Halifax. In November, the representatives concluded their talks in Toronto.

There were many events prior to the conference that pushed the three provinces to unite together. In 1862, an intercolonial railway project ran from Halifax to Quebec City. However, the Province of Canada was reluctant to pay its share. This prompted the maritime cities to unite and pay for the project together. They believed their union would increase their political strength and attract investors. Prince Edward Islanders were excited about the project, but many of the other colonies didn't share the same sentiment.

The Province of Canada was willing to create a union with the maritime colonies because it was afraid of the American invasion. The North gained so much power after the Civil War, and their "Manifest Destiny" ideas worried many Canadians. Britain also wanted to reduce its presence in North America and considered letting the U.S. take over the British colonies. The Province of Canada knew they would fall prey to the Americans if they didn't boost their power in the region. Their government was also unreliable and weak, and people had been advocating for change and a new political environment. All these factors drove the Province of Canada to create a union with the maritime colonies.

News of the Charlottetown conference reached the Canadian leaders, who found it a great opportunity to meet with other leaders and discuss their future. The Canadian government sent a representative even though they weren't on the guest list. However, he was welcomed with open arms.

Each of the maritime colonies sent five representatives. Nova Scotia sent Conservative Premier Charles Tupper, Attorney General William Alexander Henry, liberal leader Adam George Archibald, Jonathan McCully, and Robert Barry Dickey. The New Brunswick representatives were Conservative Leaders John Hamilton Gray, Edward Barron Chandler, Attorney General John Mercer Johnson, Minister William Henry Steeves, and Premiere Samuel Leonard Tilley. Prince Edward Islands sent Conservative Premier John Hamilton Gray, Edward Palmer, William Henry Pope, and liberals Andrew A. Macdonald and George Coles.

The conference brought many British colonies together, from the biggest cities to the smallest towns. The representatives of the Province of Canada used their influence to convince small maritime towns to agree to a larger and united nation. The maritime provinces had always considered a confederation with the Province of Canada, so when the opportunity presented itself, they didn't hesitate.

The Nova Scotia representatives welcomed the union as they felt it was time to unite all the colonies. John Hamilton Gray, one of the representatives of New Brunswick, was very excited about the confederation since he had been calling for it since 1849.

George Coles, one of Prince Edward Islands representatives, also welcomed the idea of a united nation. However, he had one condition: the capital should be located in Charlottetown. The representatives of the other provinces found this request to be extremely unrealistic.

After delegating for a couple of days, the Canadians invited the rest of the representatives on their ship, Queen Victoria. An amusing incident occurred that day, which showcased these men were finally on the same page. One of the Canadians said that if anyone could think of a reason these provinces shouldn't unite in holy matrimony, they should speak now or forever hold their peace. The attendees started laughing, making it clear that the Charlottetown conference was a success.

Even though they hadn't agreed on all terms yet, the laughter and amusement in the room indicated they were ready to take this step. The representatives spent the next few days delegating. The Canadians wanted the confederation to grant them full autonomy over French Canadian regions. They also made it clear that the maritime provinces only had a year to reach an agreement on the confederation. On September 7th, the Maritimes accepted the confederation's terms.

The representatives held another meeting in Quebec. They discussed various topics related to the confederation and prepared a constitution to govern all these provinces. It was necessary to make the constitution different from the Americans since the Canadians didn't want to associate with the revolutionary tone of the American constitution.

24. Sir John A. MacDonald

Sir John A. Macdonald was one of the most prominent characters in the Canadian Confederation.

Sir John A. MacDonald was one of the prominent characters in the Canadian Confederation. He was born in Scotland on January 10, 1815, and died in 1891 in Canada. He was a lawyer and the Canadian prime minister. He is often described as the father of the Canadian

Confederation. He played a huge role in the Charlottetown conference and many other conferences before finalizing the agreement. He acted as a leader for all the British colonies and proved himself during the delegations. As a result of his hard work, he was elected to be the first prime minister of the new united Canada.

During several conferences, he expressed his desire for a legislative union over a federal one. However, he realized later that a legislative system wasn't practical. He felt that it wouldn't fit the needs of Canada East, which was a minority. The inhabitants of Canada East had different nationalities, spoke different languages, and practiced different religions. They were worried that if they interacted with other Canadian cultures, they might lose their identity and history. East Canadians were very proud of their heritage and had endured prejudice and constant attacks, yet they held onto their individuality.

John realized the only solution was to abandon the hope for a confederation or create a system that would preserve each province's culture and identity. After uniting the Canadian provinces, the federal system would accommodate different regions, religions, and races.

He had no choice but to accept the federal system but insisted they should be careful, or they might end up with a federal constitution similar to the U.S. He wanted Canada to learn from America's mistakes, or they would find themselves in a civil war. During one of the confederation conferences, John explained where the U.S. went wrong. They had treated each state as a sovereign and were given more power than the general government. In Canada, all power was with the general government over the provincial governments. Rather than creating a federal province and risking repeating the U.S. mistakes, he created a "centralized federalism."

Even though this was the best option to satisfy all sides, he wasn't very pleased with it. Luckily, the imperial government recognized his genius and expertise and elected him as the first prime minister. This gave him the chance to reshape the constitution. John spent 25 years after the confederation implementing his federal system. He achieved successes such as creating a national policy, a sea-to-sea dominion, and opening up the West.

Sir John's influence still echoes to this day. He was a key figure in uniting the British colonies, contributing to Canadian institutions, and creating the Canadian school system.

Other significant figures impacted the Canadian Confederation, for example, politician George Brown, who was persistent and didn't give up until the confederation became a reality. Sir George-Étienne Cartier was another figure who guaranteed the rights of each province. These men were called the Fathers of the Confederation.

Although it didn't seem like it, women also played a role. The wives and daughters of the fathers of the confederation are called the mothers of the confederation. They attend social gatherings in Quebec, London, and Charlottetown conferences.

25. Newfoundland Joins the Confederation

In the 1860s and 1890s, the Canadian Confederation tried in every way to convince Newfoundland to join the Confederation. However, they weren't interested because they believed their future was with England and weren't associated with American colonies.

The U.S. had one of the most powerful armies in the region, and Canada feared they would invade Newfoundland. Because of this threat, Canada was willing to do everything in its power to bring Newfoundland into the confederation.

During the Great Depression, Newfoundland's economy fell apart, and the island was in a bad financial situation. They considered joining the Canadian Confederation to save themselves but weren't prepared to give up their independence. They decided the best option was to suspend their government, become a British colony, and let the country cover its debt. In 1948, after the Second World War, there were talks again about Newfoundland joining the confederation.

The people of Newfoundland were given three choices: remain under Britain's control, gain their independence, or join the Canadian Confederation.

The Newfoundlanders held an election, and about 52% voted for joining the confederation. Canada and Britain accepted Newfoundland's choice.

Newfoundland's Prime Minister Joseph Smallwood went to Ottawa to meet with Canadian Prime Minister Mackenzie King to discuss the union terms, which both parliaments approved.

In 1949, Newfoundland was the last province to join the Confederation. The island's name has changed over the years, and it's now called Newfoundland and Labrador.

The province's capital, St. John, is an ancient city and the oldest in the Confederation. For centuries, European fishermen would come to the Grand Banks shores, making the city one of the most significant in the region. After Newfoundland joined the confederation, Canada achieved its "from sea to sea" dream.

Smallwood promised the confederation to fix his country and boost the economy. This proved to be an easy task since Newfoundland benefited greatly from joining the confederation.

26. The Implications of the Canadian Confederation

The Canadian Confederation had a huge impact on Canada and the world. It achieved its dominion as a democracy and federal country. This system clearly works for Canada, as it still uses it to this day. The confederation allowed it to expand to ten provinces without shedding a drop of blood. After the Province of Canada, Nova Scotia, and New Brunswick joined the confederation, many other British colonies, like British Columbia, North-West Territories, and Manitoba, joined in. In 1898, the Yukon Territory became a part of the confederation, and in 1905, Saskatchewan and Alberta were created.

If it weren't for the confederation, Canada wouldn't be the country you see today. Centuries ago, it was divided into multiple provinces under British rule. However, many people and moments set the stage for this historical event. America's ambition spurred people living in the British Colonies into talking. Their fear of an invasion prompted them to take action to protect themselves and unite.

Many countries have come into being as a result of battles and wars. However, the Canadians only attended a few conferences, delegated, and negotiated the terms until they reached an agreement. The country needed the confederation to strengthen its economy, power, and military status to protect itself against America.

Many figures contributed to the Canadian Confederation, like Sir John MacDonald, who made Canada a federal state and made choices to protect it from civil war so it wouldn't tear the country apart. Although the confederation took place hundreds of years ago, its impact is still powerful to this day.

Chapter 6: Klondike Fever Stories

There was a time in Canadian history when the discovery of large deposits of gold in a less populated region of the country led to a massive migration of people from many other parts of the world. It was a gold rush unlike any other, and there hasn't been one as extensive or as riveting since. It has been immortalized in many books, movies, and TV shows over the years.

The Klondike Fever, or Klondike Gold Rush, as it came to be known, lasted for no more than four years, but the people involved in and affected by it felt like it went on for decades. That's how intense and harrowing their experience was. Unfortunately for many, it wasn't even rewarding in the end; of the 100,000 prospectors who had set out with dreams of laying claim to huge patches of gold deposits, only around 30,000 managed to reach the Klondike region.

However, a great many of those were greeted not with gold but with disappointment. Statistics show that only around 4,000 prospectors found and laid claim to small fields. The rest returned home empty-handed or traveled to other lands in search of another fortune. The intriguing tale of the beginning of this last great gold rush is retold in several parts of Canada and beyond to this day.

27. Skookum Jim: The Indigenous Heart of the Klondike Discovery

A Tagish native once befriended an American prospector in a cold, hard Alaskan town. What followed was a tale of trust, loyalty, family, longing, adventure, luck, prosperity, generosity, and eventual betrayal. Keish was the Tagish native's name, and the prospector was George Carmack.

Skookum Jim earned respect among packers and employers.
https://commons.wikimedia.org/wiki/File:Skookum_Jim_Mason.png

Born in 1855 to the Tagish First Nations people of Yukon, Canada, Keish grew up to become a packer, hauling provisions from the Alaskan shores to the settlements near the Yukon River. He quickly earned great respect among his fellow packers and employers, for he could carry twice the weight his peers could. This was how he came to be known as Skookum Jim. Skookum in their local language (Chinook Jargon) means strong and hardy.

Packing may have been Skookum Jim's profession, but exploration was his passion. He spent quite a while exploring and packing bacon over the Chilkoot Pass (the mountain pass that connected Alaska and Canada, which would be critical to the gold rush later) in the mid-1880s. That was where he encountered George Carmack. It didn't take long for them to become fast friends and business partners.

As George spent most of his time with Keish and his family, one thing led to another, and he became a part of that family by marrying Shaaw Tlaa, Keish's sister. She called herself Kate Carmack after marriage, and the couple stayed and prospected with Skookum Jim in Tagish for a few years. But in 1889, they left the place to seek their fortune northward, in a new town built especially for prospectors, Forty Mile.

Keish lost touch with his sister and American friend for several years when he married and had a daughter. Though he was happy in his domestic life, he longed for adventure and, more specifically, to reconnect with the Carmack family. Having had no word from Kate and George in the mid-1890s, he set out northward with his nephew, Kaa Goox, to find them. They prospected along the way but rarely found anything useful.

Toward the end of 1895, Keish and his nephew located Kate and George's lodging on the banks of the Klondike River. It was a merry reunion, especially since Skookum Jim came to know he had a niece as well (Kate and George's daughter, Graphie). After that, the family walked south from the mouth of the Klondike River down Bonanza Creek, called Rabbit Creek back then. It was somewhere there that they stumbled upon a tiny gold nugget, no larger than their pinky finger. Upon a closer look at the area, they noticed the entire basin splattered with gold.

They probably knew, at that very moment, the magnitude of their discovery, how it would make them rich beyond their dreams and spark a large-scale gold rush. But they were too busy with the politics and ethics of the situation. Back in the day, racism ran rampant in the world, so much so that George was treated harshly by his fellow Americans just for mingling with the indigenous tribes. It is said that Skookum Jim laid eyes on the gold nugget before anyone else. Ethics dictated that he should be rightly credited for the discovery.

However, the local authorities may not have recognized the claim of a tribal individual. Hence, the discoverers decided that George would take the credit for the discovery. It is possible that Kate Carmack first discovered the nugget, but only three claims were made on the Klondike gold fields and the surrounding territories, those of George, Keish, and Kaa Goox (the nephew). If she didn't even get her share of the gold, letting her take the credit for the discovery probably hadn't even entered their minds. It was just another day in a woman's life in the 1800s.

Skookum Jim changed drastically when he got his hands on the gold, mostly for the better. He may have veered away from his Tagish roots, but he didn't hesitate to share his wealth with his family and his people. George Carmack changed as well – but for worse. He left Kate to fend for herself, moved to Seattle, United States, and married a local. Keish rescued his sister by building her a grand cabin near his house.

Alas, it is said that good people are often hit with one misfortune after another. Skookum Jim developed a drinking habit in his later years that destroyed his marriage and, eventually, his life. But he was mindful enough to secure his family's future by opening a trust under his daughter's name, the Daisy Mason Trust.

28. The Golden Staircase: Tales of the Chilkoot Pass

One of humankind's biggest gold rushes began soon after Skookum Jim and his companions discovered the gold deposits along the Klondike River in August 1896. However, miners living in towns nearby had already claimed all the fields in Bonanza Creek. The larger deposits lay in another place, the Eldorado Creek, just south of the original discovery bank. By the time prospectors found them, news had reached Circle City in Alaska, a few hundred miles northwest of Klondike.

It was December, and prospectors looking to have a prosperous Christmas arrived in Klondike in droves, hoping to lay their claims. But it wasn't until June of the following year (1897) that the rest of the world learned about the new-found gold deposits. That was when the gold rush truly began.

Many thousands set out from Seattle and San Francisco in the United States on ships through fierce, cold winds, bearing several heavy sacks of supplies each. Those who landed at Dyea, a small Alaskan town largely abandoned today, had to traverse the Chilkoot Pass to reach the gold deposits in and around Klondike. Animals bore their heavy burdens for the first few miles, a steady upslope that passed through camps of fellow prospectors and natives looking to make a living.

But there came a point in their trail that animals could not cross. It was a steep ledge that led to the actual climb, the base of which was called the Scales. There, the trekkers left their beasts and checked in their luggage to officially enter Canada from the US. It was the point after which the "stampeders," as they later came to be known, faced their true test.

The Chilkoot Pass was like an initiation ritual for the aspiring and established gold miners. Only those who were hardy enough to pass it were worthy of claiming their share of gold. Not that there weren't other easier ways into the Klondike, but this was probably the fastest route. And as all previous gold rushes had proven, the quicker they reached the gold deposits, the better their chances were of staking a claim on the more valuable fields. Indeed, over 22,000 people attempted to scale the Pass during the rush.

The Chilkoot Trail was a 33-mile long, dangerous, snow-covered path that led to the shores of Lake Bennett, a place where they could find some respite from their tedious climb. The trek was made even harder by the Canadian officials who advised the stampeders to carry a year's worth of supplies (which weighed close to a ton) since there wasn't enough food to be found beyond that point. It meant the travelers had to make multiple trips up and down the Pass.

The steep ledge beyond the Scales was a thousand feet of backbreaking climb that often took more than a day to climb. Cataclysmic avalanches were common, one of which claimed the lives of 60 stampeders. Only the super-wealthy could make it up in a single trip by hiring multiple local packers, who charged up to a dollar per pound.

As the months progressed and winter made way for summer, the incoming stampeders devised several ways to ease their journey. A crude but effective move in the early stages was constructing steps to reduce most of the risks associated with the climb. These 1500 steps eventually became known as the Golden Staircase, a kind of tribute to the gold that lay in wait for those who managed to climb it. It helped many travelers reach Lake Bennett without mishap.

However, the main drawback of this staircase was its width. Two people abreast could not climb together, so the stampeders had to slog in a single file. This prompted another one of the travelers to build a more efficient means of transportation, the tramway. The first tramways in 1897 were primitive. A simple rope connected the beginning of the Pass to the top, and it carried makeshift sleds. The contraption was operated by a running horse that rotated a wheel that pulled the rope.

It didn't take them long to upgrade to steam-powered and aerial tramways, and by 1898, many of the semi-rich prospectors could traverse the Chilkoot Pass quickly and comfortably (the rate was no more than 30 cents per pound).

29. Dead Horse Trail: Tales of the White Pass

Dyea was not the only port for the prospectors to alight at the nearest Klondike. The town of Skagway, a few miles east of Dyea, offered an easier route to the gold deposits than the Chilkoot Pass. It was called the White Pass. Its presence was closely guarded by the natives until the Canadian explorer William Ogilvie uncovered it in 1887.

During the Klondike Gold Rush, several thousand prospectors landed at Skagway port and proceeded toward the White Pass, their pack horses in tow. It was a more or less even path through the Coast Mountains, and the snow bathed it in white all around, hence the name. The elements barely provided any resistance to the travelers in the beginning. However, as the trail wore on, it became narrower and narrower until the path became no wider than a couple of feet, with a looming mountain on one side and a series of jagged rock formations on the other.

That was where the travelers' horses began panicking, and one after the other, they slipped and fell over the edge and were skewered upon the sharp rocks. It is said that more than 3,000 horses died this way, and White Pass came to be called the Dead Horse Trail.

Since prospectors entered the pass in great numbers, it didn't take long for the traffic to get clogged in the narrow regions. That was why the Canadian authorities closed the White Pass near the end of 1897, after which several thousand travelers were marooned at Skagway like rats in a sack. Thankfully, the authorities recognized the precariousness of the situation well before it escalated, and they built a separate toll road leading to the gold deposits in 1898.

In the throes of winter, the conditions became even harsher. Despite the new road, the travelers suffered greatly on the way to their destination, primarily due to the Soapy Smith gang. This band of native thugs repeatedly depleted the resources of the travelers until the latter had to survive on horse meat from their skewered remains back in 1897. Soapy Smith's leader was eventually killed in 1898, but the damage had been done.

Only a small number of prospectors managed to reach the Yukon River that led to the Klondike gold fields. The rest returned to Skagway empty-handed, most of whom suffered from severe mental issues later.

30. Dawson City: From Wilderness to Boomtown

In the early 1800s, the area known today as Dawson City was nothing but a wild wasteland at the mercy of the Han-speaking natives of the Klondike region. From a bare hunting ground, it emerged as an important landmark during the Klondike Gold Rush, thanks to Joseph Ladue, a then-small prospector in the Yukon Territory. He was one of the first to reach the Klondike region after Skookum Jim and his companions discovered the massive gold deposits. It enabled him to lay claim to around 170 acres of gold-beset land.

Unlike most of the other prospectors, Ladue was a true-blue businessman. He didn't settle for his gold claims. He possessed the art of foresight. Imagining the land he owned as a potential stop-off point for the inevitable gold rush, he built a residential town there, naming it after the reputable Canadian geologist of his time, George Mercer Dawson. Indeed, it transformed from a tiny encampment of natives in 1896 to a thriving town of over 16,000 gold-obsessed migrants in just two years.

The population kept rising near the middle of 1898 until it peaked at the end of the year. It so happened that the Dawson City region wasn't equipped to handle a large number of people. From the rapidly depleting drinking water to the scarcity of purchasable plots, it seemed that only the gold deposits around the region held it together.

After the Klondike Gold Rush came to an abrupt end in 1899, the population in Dawson City was also depleted (from over 30,000 to less than 8,000). Other elemental factors came to the fore, like the incessant floods throughout the early 1900s, and its population reduced even further. Today, Dawson City is more of a historical landmark, housing a little more than 1500 residents.

31. The Cure for the Klondike Fever

Klondike Fever may have wrapped the world in its embrace like a serpent rapidly coiling around its prey. But it relinquished its hold quite easily. By the time Klondike became more accessible with the development of advanced tramways and railway routes in 1898, the gold sources were largely depleted, and the gold rush had run out of steam.

A considerable number of prospectors were traditionally inclined. The raw method of mining the gold in a coarse, underdeveloped environment mattered more to them than the value of the metal itself. The Klondike Gold Rush brought about rapid cultural and technological developments in Dawson City. The late lamented hunting ground had become a tourist hub, from billiards and pool tables to exotic dining menus. Even the fashion sense of the locals had evolved to depict the then-modern fads. That was when many passion-focused prospectors lost interest in the Klondike fields.

The major reason for the Klondike decline was the discovery of another base of gold deposits southward, near Atlin Lake. But the ultimate cure to the fever proved to be a larger deposit in the Alaskan town of Nome. Initially, a small number of prospectors trickled down from Dawson to Nome.

Those miners who lingered in Dawson City, hoping to reignite the rush, eventually realized that the price of their stay had begun exceeding the profits made from their goldfield claims. The Spanish-American war in the spring of 1898 added fuel to the fire, and many of them eventually left in large numbers during the summer, either to go back home or search for some other fortune.

The nail in the coffin of the Klondike Gold Rush was hammered in August 1899, when over 2,500 prospectors in Dawson City left the then unprofitable place for the booming town of Nome. The world media stirred up the flames of the declining gold quantities in Klondike, from spouting sarcastic gold rush quotes regarding the region to making headlines out of other lesser kinds of news.

Indeed, by September 1899, Klondike Fever had become a part of history. It was an important part of that history, as several media sources have repeatedly proved over the years. From the earliest silent movies like The Gold Rush (1925) starring Charlie Chaplin to the latest creations like Dathaí Keane's An Klondike (2015-2017). It was immortalized in obscure nonfiction novels like Jack London's The Call of the Wild and popular comics based on the quintessential fictional gold king, Scrooge McDuck.

It goes without saying that the Klondike Fever may have been cured a long time ago, but its effects resonate in the lives of the common folk time and again to this day.

Chapter 7: Canada's Sacrifice: Accounts from World War I

The First World War, often called World War I, was a global conflict that reshaped history in the early 20th century. While it involved many nations, Canada's involvement in the war was a defining moment in its history. Some moments define nations, where the collective will and courage of a people are put to the ultimate test; such a moment emerged for Canada during World War I. As the world plunged into the depths of the Great War, Canada, as part of the British Empire, was thrust into a global conflict it had not sought but would ultimately embrace with unwavering resolve. From the battlefields of Europe to the home front, Canadians played a crucial role in the war effort, and their sacrifices were felt by their fellow countrymen and the entire world.

32. Canada's Call to Arms: The Nation's Entry into WWI

The assassination of Archduke Franz Ferdinand of Austria-Hungary on June 28, 1914, served as the catalyst for the outbreak of World War I. The subsequent chain reaction of alliances and declarations of war by European nations drew Canada into the conflict. When Britain declared war on Germany on August 4, 1914, Canada was automatically at war as a dominion of the British Empire. This declaration marked the formal beginning of Canada's involvement in World War I.

Canada's initial involvement was largely a result of its obligations and commitments as a member of the Empire. Canada recognized the importance of maintaining British interests and defending the Empire. Many Canadians felt a sense of duty to support Britain in its time of need, viewing the conflict as a just cause and a way to preserve the values and way of life associated with the British Empire.

Canada also had significant economic interests tied to Britain and Europe. Trade with these regions was vital to the Canadian economy, and a stable Europe was essential for continued prosperity. Disruption of trade routes and economic stability due to the war threatened Canada's economic well-being.

Sir Robert Borden offered full support to Britain.
https://commons.wikimedia.org/wiki/File:Sir_Robert_Borden.jpg

In the early days of the war, there was a surge of patriotism and enthusiasm among Canadians. Many believed the war would be short-lived and that Canadian troops would return home as heroes. Recruitment offices nationwide were inundated with volunteers eager to join the fight. The Canadian government, led by the Prime Minister. Sir Robert Borden was quick to offer full support to Britain. Borden pledged substantial troops and resources to aid the British war effort.

The Canadian public largely supported this stance, and political opposition to the war was minimal.

Canada quickly mobilized its military forces. In October 1914, the 1st Canadian contingent sailed for Europe. These troops and subsequent contingents played a vital role in various battles and campaigns on the Western Front. First came the Battle of Ypres, which took place in the Ypres Salient, a section of the Western Front in Belgium. It was one of the earliest battles of World War I and was marked by the Germans' first large-scale use of poison gas.

Canadian forces, specifically the 1st Canadian Division, were stationed in the Ypres Salient. They faced the brunt of the German gas attacks. The Germans released chlorine gas on April 22, 1915, creating a green-yellow cloud that drifted towards the Canadian lines. The gas caused panic and significant casualties among the unprepared troops. The Canadian soldiers' courage in the face of the gas attack and their efforts to plug the gaps in the line became legendary. They withstood further gas attacks and fierce German assaults, preventing a complete breakthrough.

Then came the Battle of the Somme, a massive Allied offensive launched on the Western Front, primarily in the region of the River Somme in France. It was intended to relieve pressure on the French forces, who were suffering heavy casualties at Verdun. The battle commenced on July 1, 1916, and lasted until November. Canadian forces, part of the British Expeditionary Force, were tasked with capturing the village of Courcelette and the surrounding area. The Canadian Corps, under the command of Lieutenant-General Julian Byng, played a pivotal role in this operation.

33. Vimy Ridge: Birthplace of a Nation

Fast-forward to the spring of 1917, and the Canadian Corps faced one of its greatest challenges: Vimy Ridge. The Ridge, a formidable German stronghold, had defied all previous Allied attempts at capture. It consisted of a high escarpment overlooking a wide expanse of flat ground, providing the Germans with a commanding view of the surrounding area. This vantage point allowed them to observe and target Allied troop movements, making it a significant obstacle to the Allies' advance. Vimy Ridge was also a vital part of the German defensive system known as the Hindenburg Line, a series of heavily fortified positions designed to resist any Allied offensive. Capturing Vimy Ridge was crucial for the Allied forces, as it would eliminate a major threat and open up opportunities for further advances.

The Canadian Corps, led by Lieutenant-General Sir Julian Byng, was tasked with capturing Vimy Ridge. The Canadian soldiers were highly motivated and well-trained, and their leaders recognized the need for meticulous planning and coordination. The Canadians employed tunneling and mining techniques to create a network of underground tunnels and chambers. This provided protection from enemy fire and allowed troops to approach the ridge unseen. A carefully planned artillery barrage preceded the infantry assault. Canadian gunners had mapped out German positions with remarkable precision, ensuring the enemy's defenses would be significantly weakened by the time the infantry advanced. Canadian commanders developed innovative tactics, including using "creeping barrages" to provide covering fire as the infantry advanced. They also introduced the "rolling barrage," a technique that allowed artillery to move in sync with the advancing infantry.

The battle commenced at 5:30 a.m. on April 9, 1917, with a massive artillery barrage that pounded the German defenses. The Canadian infantry, equipped with rifles and bayonets, began their advance through the mist and smoke, determined to take Vimy Ridge. The Canadian soldiers faced numerous challenges, including heavy machine gun fire and fierce German resistance. However, their training, discipline, and determination enabled them to push forward. Over several days, the Canadians made significant progress. On April 12, 1917, they triumphantly captured Vimy Ridge. The victory was not without sacrifice, as Canadian forces suffered over 10,000 casualties, including nearly 3,600 killed.

The success at Vimy Ridge was a unifying moment for Canada. It was the first time all four Canadian divisions had fought together as a cohesive force, transcending regional and linguistic divisions. This achievement contributed to a growing sense of Canadian identity and nationhood. The experiences of Canadian soldiers at Vimy Ridge were both heroic and harrowing. They endured the horrors of trench warfare, witnessed the devastation caused by artillery, and faced the constant threat of gas attacks. Despite these challenges, they displayed remarkable courage and resilience.

Soldiers endured the grim realities of trench warfare, including exposure to the elements, infestations of rats, and the ever-present danger of snipers. The Germans frequently used poison gas during the battle, leading to Canadian troops developing and using gas masks. One notable figure was Private John George Pattison, who earned the Victoria Cross for his courageous actions in capturing a machine gun position.

The Battle of Vimy Ridge left an enduring legacy that continues to shape Canada's national identity and its place in the world. Vimy Ridge is often referred to as the "birthplace of a nation." It marked a pivotal moment in Canada's history, where its soldiers fought under a common flag and forged a sense of unity and purpose. To commemorate the battle, Canada erected the Vimy Memorial, a stunning monument designed by Walter Allward, on the ridge itself. The memorial stands as a symbol of Canadian sacrifice and resilience.

Canada's success at Vimy Ridge helped establish the country's reputation for peacekeeping and diplomacy. In the aftermath of World War I, Canada played a significant role in the League of Nations, a precursor to the United Nations, promoting international cooperation and conflict resolution.

34. Passchendaele: The Battle in the Mud

The Battle of Passchendaele, also known as the Third Battle of Ypres, was one of the most grueling and infamous battles of World War I. Fought from July 31 to November 10, 1917, in the Ypres Salient in Belgium, it is remembered for its relentless rain, thick mud, and the tremendous human cost incurred by both sides. The Ypres Salient was a bulge in the Western Front held by the Germans. It was strategically important due to its proximity to the Belgian ports, which the British desperately needed for supply lines. Capturing Passchendaele Ridge was a key objective because it gave the Allies a vantage point to monitor German positions and control the surrounding landscape.

One of the defining characteristics of the Battle of Passchendaele was the relentless rain. The region experienced unusually heavy rainfall during the summer and fall of 1917, transforming the battlefield into a quagmire of mud and waterlogged craters. This constant deluge made movement difficult and exacerbated the misery for soldiers. The trenches on both sides were often knee-deep in mud. Soldiers had to contend with enemy fire and the challenges posed by the mud, which made it difficult to traverse, limited mobility, and created unsanitary conditions. Trench foot, a painful condition caused by prolonged exposure to wet and cold conditions, became a widespread problem.

The Battle of Passchendaele saw some of the most intense artillery bombardments of the war. The constant shelling churned the ground, creating even more mud and further complicating troop movements. Soldiers on both sides endured the horrors of trench life in appalling conditions. The mud, cold, and constant threat of enemy fire took a toll on their physical and mental well-being.

The Battle of Passchendaele resulted in staggering casualties. Canadian and British forces, among others, suffered tremendous losses. The Germans also suffered heavy casualties as the battle went on. Canadian and British forces suffered significant casualties during the battle, reporting over 15,000 casualties, including over 4,000 killed. British losses were similarly staggering, with many soldiers falling victim to the brutal conditions and enemy fire.

Despite the harsh conditions, there were numerous acts of valor and heroism. Soldiers displayed unwavering courage as they pressed forward, under fire through the muck. The Battle of Passchendaele saw several soldiers earn the Victoria Cross, the highest military decoration for valor. Among them was Private Robert Hanna of the Canadian Expeditionary Force. On August 21, 1917, during a fierce attack, Hanna rushed a machine gun position single-handedly, capturing the gun and its crew. His courageous action inspired his comrades to continue the advance.

Another notable act of valor came from Lieutenant Hugh McKenzie, a Canadian officer. On October 30, 1917, during intense fighting, McKenzie led his men in an assault on an enemy strongpoint. Despite being wounded, he continued to encourage his troops until he was mortally wounded.

Private James Peter Robertson of the Canadian Expeditionary Force was another Victoria Cross recipient. On October 26, 1917, he volunteered for a dangerous mission to rescue wounded comrades while under heavy machine guns and artillery fire. His extraordinary courage and determination saved many lives.

35. The Home Front: Women, War Bonds, and Conscription Controversy

World War I was a war that deeply affected not only the soldiers on the front lines but also the civilians on the home front. While Canadian soldiers fought valiantly overseas, a different kind of battle unfolded on the home front. Women, traditionally confined to domestic roles, stepped into the breach left by their loved ones at the front lines. They took on factory jobs, tended to the wounded, and provided essential support to the war effort.

As the war intensified, the demand for labor and resources increased significantly. Women played a crucial role in filling the void left by men who had gone to fight. They entered the workforce in large numbers, taking on jobs previously held by men, including working in munitions factories, hospitals, and offices. Their contributions were essential in maintaining the country's industrial and economic output.

Women also made substantial contributions through volunteer work. Organizations like the Red Cross and the Canadian Patriotic Fund mobilized women to knit socks, sew uniforms, and provide support to soldiers. This voluntary effort boosted morale and had practical implications in terms of supplying essential goods for the troops.

The war created an opportunity for the women's suffrage movement in Canada. In 1917, women in Manitoba, Alberta, and Saskatchewan gained the right to vote in provincial elections, and the federal government extended voting rights to women who were closely related to military personnel. These changes were seen as a recognition of women's contributions to the war effort.

On the other hand, war bonds were introduced to finance the war effort, known as war loan drives. These drives encouraged citizens to invest their money in government bonds to help fund the war. Canadians responded enthusiastically, purchasing bonds in large numbers. The money raised through these bonds financed various aspects of the war, from purchasing equipment for the military to building infrastructure for the war effort. The sale of war bonds raised money for the war and stimulated the Canadian economy. The increased demand for goods and services generated economic growth and helped Canada recover from a recession that had plagued the country before the war. The purchase of war bonds was seen as a patriotic duty, and Canadians took great pride in contributing to the war effort in this way. Schools, businesses, and community groups organized bond-buying drives, creating a sense of unity and shared responsibility among the civilian population.

Then came the issue of conscription, or mandatory military service, which was one of the most divisive and contentious debates on the Canadian home front during World War I. As the war dragged on, the need for more troops became apparent. Canadian forces had suffered heavy casualties, and it became increasingly difficult to maintain a volunteer-based army. Prime Minister Sir Robert Borden's government, recognizing the necessity of more manpower, proposed conscription in 1917.

The introduction of conscription caused a deep rift in Canadian society. English-speaking Canadians and those from urban areas generally supported conscription, as they felt a greater connection to the British Empire. In contrast, French Canadians, particularly in Quebec, were largely opposed to conscription. They viewed the war as a European conflict and felt little allegiance to the British Empire. The conscription crisis had significant political repercussions. It led to the formation of the Union Government, a coalition of pro-conscription Liberals and Conservatives that sought to address the divisions within the country. Borden's decision to introduce conscription also caused a split in the Liberal Party, with many French Canadian Liberals opposing the measure.

Opposition to conscription resulted in protests and even riots in certain parts of the country, particularly in Quebec. In 1918, the conscription issue escalated when riots broke out in Quebec City and Montreal. The military was called in to restore order, further exacerbating tensions. The conscription crisis left a lasting impact on Canadian national unity. The divide between English-speaking and French-speaking Canadians deepened, and the scars of the conscription debates persisted long after the war ended.

36. Aftermath: Canada in the Post-War World

November 11, 1918, signaled the end of World War I, a conflict that had exacted an enormous toll on Canada. It was a day of both relief and reflection as the nation emerged from the war forever changed. For Canada, the cost of World War I was staggering. Over 61,000 Canadians had lost their lives in the conflict, while tens of thousands more returned home wounded or permanently disabled. The nation mourned the loss of a generation of young men and women, and nearly every community in Canada was touched by the grief of bereaved families.

The physical and psychological toll on returning soldiers was immense. Many soldiers came back with physical injuries, ranging from amputations to disfigurements. The war has also exposed soldiers to unimaginable horrors, leading to a widespread prevalence of post-traumatic stress disorder (PTSD), though it was not formally recognized at the time. The psychological scars of battle haunted veterans for years. The war left a mark on Canadian families. Mothers, fathers, wives, and children grieved for their loved ones who never returned or returned forever changed. The loss of breadwinners and caregivers placed enormous burdens on families, leading to economic hardships and social upheaval.

Despite the heavy toll of the war, Canada emerged as a respected global player. The sacrifices made by Canadian soldiers earned the nation a seat at the table during the negotiations for the Treaty of Versailles, which formally ended the state of war between the Allies and Germany. Canada's presence at this historic diplomatic event signaled a significant departure from its colonial past. It was no longer just a dominion within the British Empire but a sovereign nation recognized as a valuable international partner. The war profoundly influenced Canada's identity. The sacrifices made by its citizens in the trenches of Europe and on other battlefronts fostered a sense of unity and purpose. The nation had proven itself on the global stage, and its people had demonstrated resilience and determination. Canada was no longer seen merely as a British outpost but as a nation capable of independently defending its values and interests.

The legacy of World War I lingered in Canada for generations. The grief of families who had lost loved ones remained palpable, and communities across the country established war memorials to honor the fallen. November 11th, known as Remembrance Day in Canada, became a solemn occasion for Canadians to remember and pay tribute to those who had made the ultimate sacrifice. The experience of the war, along with the post-war economic challenges, contributed to social changes, including the emergence of a stronger labor movement and the recognition of women's contributions to the workforce, which eventually led to women's suffrage.

November 11, 1918, marked the end of World War I, but for Canada, it was the beginning of a new chapter. The war's toll, in terms of casualties, physical and psychological traumas, and its impact on families, was immense and enduring. Yet, the sacrifices of Canadian soldiers had earned the nation a newfound status on the world stage and reshaped its national identity. The legacy of the war persisted through generations, serving as a reminder of the profound impact of conflict on individuals and societies and the resilience and unity that can emerge in its wake.

Chapter 8: Stories from the Avro Arrow Saga

Avro Canada, a Canadian aircraft manufacturing company, worked on developing a revolutionary, all-whether, supersonic fighter interceptor called the CF-105 Arrow, or Avro Arrow, between 1952 and 1959. The aircraft had a futuristic, sleek design and was equipped with technologies that were ahead of its time. This aircraft represented the dreams, vision, and deduction of Canadian engineers until its abrupt end. Avro Canada was founded in 1945 and became among the 100 top companies in the world by 1958.

Reading this chapter, you'll learn about the significance of this ambitious project. You'll understand the Avro Arrow and learn about its intended role and advanced technological features. This chapter explores the development of the project and the political and financial challenges that led to its cancellation. It also covers the controversy surrounding this event and the consequences that followed.

37. The Avro Arrow

The Avro CF-105 was a turning point in the world of aerospace projects and technologies.
Clemens Vasters from Viersen, Germany, Germany, CC BY 2.0
<*https://creativecommons.org/licenses/by/2.0*>, *via Wikimedia Commons:*
https://commons.wikimedia.org/wiki/File:Avro_Canada_CF-105_Arrow_(34434072144).jpg

The development of the Avro CF-105 was a turning point in the world of aerospace projects and technologies on an international scale. This aircraft, developed to defend the nation against the Soviet Union's attacks, was a significant evolution in aerodynamics and engine design. It was among the first aircraft to incorporate a fly-by-wire flight control system, which uses computer-assisted flight technology and sensors to improve responsive controls and stability. Its creation also redefined the framework of engine design, warranting supersonic speed and sophisticated design. Even though the project gained widespread attention from the public and press, it was eventually canceled in 1959.

The creation of this state-of-the-art aircraft and the accompanying intricate technology created a lot of job opportunities for skilled workers, technicians, engineers, and pilots. This project shed light on the numerous talents, innovative ideas, and skilled individuals in Canada's aviation industry. Despite its high costs, the public was excited about the project and wasn't skeptical.

During the 1940s, the Union of Soviet Socialist Republics, the USSR, threatened Canada's welfare. The USSR's increasing threat triggered the onset of the Cold War, and political relations between the Soviet Union and the United States were compromised during the 1950s. There was reason to believe that the UUSR would eventually attack the U.S. by attacking the Canadian Arctic with bombs. Canada was inadvertently caught in the crossfire due to its geographic location and political stance. In response to these expectations, Canada built the Avro CF-1o5.

38. Breaking Barriers: The Design and Innovation of the Avro Arrow

Crawford Gordon Jr., the director of the wartime defense production, James C. Floyd, a distinguished English engineer, and Janusz Zurakowski, a Polish fighter pilot, alongside other remarkable figures, came together to develop this incredible aeronautical innovation.

The Avro Arrow was an ambitious project to take on at the time. The interceptor aircraft weighed 22,240kg when empty, was 24m long, and had a 15m wingspan. The Avro Arrow was designed to be sleek yet fully functional. In addition to being among the first aircraft to incorporate computer-assisted flight control technology, it housed the first computerized weapons system. The aircraft was the fastest of its kind, traveling almost twice the speed of sound at 53,000ft high. The development of this monumental project showcased the exceptional skills and dedication of the Canadian engineers involved. Their vision and execution left a permanent mark on the aviation industry.

There was no computer simulation equipment at the time, making the testing process very exacting. Wind tunnels and scale models were used to conduct intensive testing procedures. Nine models, around 12.5% percent the size of the actual planes, were tested on rockets that flew over Lake Ontario, and two others went over the Atlantic Ocean.

The first revelation of the aircraft took place at the Avro plant on the 4th of October 1957. The first few thousand spectators were astounded by the grandeur of the plane. However, on the same day the aircraft was revealed to the public, the Soviet Union happened to launch Sputnik 1, which was the world's first satellite. It was an equally exciting event that overshadowed the press coverage of the unveiling of the Avro Arrow. While it wasn't the deciding factor, this event and its ramifications played a role in the cancelation of the aircraft program later.

The project was under much pressure to perform, mainly due to its high costs. Many critics also wondered if the intercept would carry outdated technology in a few years, worrying that manned aircraft would become a thing of the past. The reporter for the Hamilton Spectator explained that the interceptor could easily demolish Russian bombers but wondered whether it could stand the test of time and effectively defend against advanced rocket missiles at its launch in 1961.

Zurakowski piloted its first flight around five months later, breaking several speed records. Five models of the first version of the plane were manufactured, which flew 66 times throughout 1958. The first test flight, according to Zurakowski, was simple. All he had to do was check that all the components, engines, and controls were operating and responding as they should. He tested how the plane would handle a speed of 460 mph and a lower speed while landing. The second version of the plane, which was still being developed at the time, never flew.

39. The Black Friday: The Abrupt End of a Dream

In 1957, a Progressive Conservative government was elected, replacing the long-standing liberal rule. Diefenbaker, the new Canadian Prime Minister, prioritized cutting government spending under this regime. Being an expensive venture, Avro Arrow's cost was likely a contributing cause to its cancellation. The program cost $1.1 billion, which was considered a lot for a nation of Canada's size.

Before its cancelation, the Avro Arrow had checked all the boxes on the country's defense policy, becoming the world's most popular interceptor. Canada and other countries in the North American Aerospace Defense Command (NORAD) were primarily concerned about the Soviet Union's bomber attack threats. Therefore, the Royal Canadian Air Force (RCAF) was searching for a fighter that could operate under specific, strenuous circumstances. For instance, it had to operate effectively at an altitude of 50,000, a speed that is at least 1.5 times faster than the speed of sound, and be equipped with advanced missiles.

Specialized engines and flying control systems were developed for this purpose, and the first version of the arrow, which flew out in March 1958, proved to be the best interceptor. Unsurprisingly, the aircraft attracted the attention of enthusiasts and relevant political parties worldwide. Some saw the Arrow as an opportunity to transform the aviation industry, and others, such as the U.S., worried it was a threat to their national aircraft sector. The U.S. was also working on new interceptors at the time, which made them even more interested in the Avro Arrow. That said, Americans had little faith in the practicality of the project.

Canada Faces Pressure by the U.S.

The cost of the project gradually decreased as it showed its incredible potential. Now that the Avro Arrow was tangible, it competed with other aircraft of its kind. American aircraft engineers feared the moment that their projects would compete with the Arrow, encouraging its cancellation. The U.S. didn't show interest in the Avro Arrow because they wanted to buy it, but rather to gather information about it and its engine, Iroquois.

The U.S. used this information to develop the Semi-Automatic Ground Environment (SAGE) and Boeing Michigan Aeronautical Research Center (BOMARC) system to end the Avro Arrow. The SAGE was a computerized system that could detect, track, and intercept enemy missiles and aircraft. The BOMARC was a surface-to-air missile system that was equipped with nuclear warheads.

Canada didn't have proof of the effectiveness of the BOMARC systems but was pressured to buy them anyway. In August 1958, George Pearkes, Canada's Defense Minister, was told that the U.S. would install the system near the south of the Great Lakes if Canada didn't accept the offer. Positioning the BOMARCs at this location signaled nuclear threats over Ontario. Canada had no choice but to buy the BOMARC, which meant they couldn't afford the Avro Arrow.

While the end of the Arrow disappointed many, buying the BOMARCs proved to be a good bargain for Canada. It was a more cost-effective way to defend against manned bombers. The system was also capable of both intercepting and neutralizing enemy aircraft, reducing the need for around 100 aircraft in Canada's Defense System. The U.S. was also willing to cover the majority of the cost for Canada to acquire the BOMARC missile system, making it an attractive offer.

Aside from the fear of competing with the Avro Arrow, the U.S. worried that this interceptor, the only one designed to operate at an altitude of 60,000 to 70,000 ft, would discover the U.S.'s spying mission. The U.S. flew two spy planes at 70,000 ft high to gather information about the Soviets. If the Soviet Union had found out about it, they would've immediately shot down the planes and used it as evidence that the U.S. was trying to invade the country.

The U.S. carefully considered the time of the cancellation, ensuring that versions of the plane that carried the Iroquois engines hadn't gone on any flights yet. They also acquired the aircraft's manufacturing data before shutting down the project, allowing them to develop more advanced technologies.

The Revelation of Underestimated Costs

After Canada couldn't sell the Avro Arrow, international interest in the interceptor died down, leading to its demise. While the Royal Air Force (RAF) and the United States Air Force (USAF) were both up-to-speed on the project, C.D. Howe, the Canadian Minister of Trade and Commerce at the time, had underestimated the cost of $100 million. This meant that the program would cost around $335 million. Not to mention that the unit cost for producing the small number of 100 aircraft required by Canada would be much higher than the unit cost of manufacturing similar aircraft in the U.S. After factoring in all of these considerations, the total project cost would have been $780 million, which was significantly higher than the initial estimate. By the time the project was canceled, it had already used up 97% of its budget, adding more financial strain on the Canadian government. Mr. Pearkes decided that the BOMARC was a more economical way to defend the country against the manned bomb threat and canceled the Avro Arrow project on February 23, 1959.

The Black Friday

The day of cancellation became known as "Black Friday." Mr. Pearkes explained that financial challenges weren't the only reason the program ended and that it was also due to pressure from the U.S. This project had allowed Canada to lead the aviation industry, as it would benefit all NATO countries. However, Diefenbaker believed that carrying through with the project was a liberal initiative, which went against everything that the current government stood for.

Diefenbaker knew that announcing the cancellation would lead to an uproar, which is why he used propaganda to spread the word that there were ballistic missile threats rather than manned bombers. He could introduce the BOMBARC missiles as a more effective defense solution. To make the cancellation appear more convincing, he set a faux test in motion, showing the Arrow to be significantly weaker than it was. He then canceled the project right before the assembly of the aircraft.

Despite his reasoning, it was generally known that a supersonic interceptor was the best way to neutralize advanced manned bombers. Yet, he ended up buying the BOMBARC systems to defend against manned bombers, which was ironic.

After the Avro Arrow was canceled, Canada signed NORAD and defense-sharing agreements that stated that the nation would no longer develop advanced aircraft, leaving weapon and engine development in the hands of the U.S. This forced the Royal Canadian Air Force (RCAF) to spend billions of dollars on fighters developed by either the U.S. or Britain.

More than 14,000 skilled engineers and aviation professionals were out of work, causing many Canadians in the aerospace industry to migrate to the U.S. and Great Britain. Many top Canadian engineers worked on the Concorde civil airliner, while others worked at NASA, contributing to one of the most significant events in world history: sending the first man to the moon.

By July 1959, all the designs, models, machinery, plans, studies, and blueprints used to develop the Avro Arrow were destroyed. Blowtorches were also used to tear down all versions of their aircraft, and their scraps were sold to junk dealers for as little as 6.5 cents per pound.

Diefenbaker responded to criticism defiantly for years after the cancellation. He repeatedly explained that even though he felt distressed about canceling the project, it was necessary. In one interview, he said that the Avro Arrow was a beautiful, impressive aircraft and that canceling the program and facing the consequential criticism and attacks required great strength. The government's need to cancel the program and erase its technical data from history is still questioned to this day.

The Aftermath of the Cancellation

In addition to purchasing the BOMARC systems, Canada bought 66 Voodoo fighter jets from the fighter jets. Not only were they second-hand aircraft, but they were also more than 0.5 times slower than the Arrow. Interestingly, the combined cost of the BOMARC systems and Voodoo fighter jets that Canada purchased amounted to more than what the Avro Arrow program would've cost.

By this time, a growing anti-nuclear sentiment was spreading throughout the Canadian public. Expressing their strong aversion toward nuclear weapons and nuclear-related activities, the public encouraged the government to call for the end of the arms race and remove its armed forces from all nuclear activities. Canada also eventually shut down the BOMARC system.

Gordon, the president of Avro Canada, resigned in July 1959 and died eight years later. Fred Smye, the company's vice president at the time, also resigned in 1959. The company was dissolved three years later, and its assets were sold for $15.6 million. While Canada's modern-day aviation industry is performing reasonably well, the Avro Arrow cancelation left short- and long-term implications on Canada's economic and political performance.

If the project hadn't been canceled, Canada's aerospace sector would've likely benefited from the technical data and expertise of the skilled scientists who sought employment in other countries. The cancellation also left lasting effects on research and development in the nation's aerospace industry.

40. Legacy of the Lost Arrow: Canada's Aerospace Industry after the Avro

Fortunately, the remnants of this legendary project are not all lost. You can find some of the original Arrow's components, replicas, and scaled models of the project in several Canadian museums today. For instance, the Canada Aviation and Space Museum displays the largest surviving component of the original Arrow: its nose. You'll also see the devastating words "cut here" where it was blowtorched. The Canadian Air and Space Conservancy is also home to a full-size replica of the aircraft.

A group of scientists, businessmen, and historians recently searched Lake Ontario for remnants of the aircraft and discovered a relevant object in 2017, which turned out to be a small test device of the earlier Arrow scale models. They decided to continue the search using underwater sonar equipment, collecting data, and identifying thousands of objects. They discovered a debris field and found the largest piece of the model in 2020.

Blueprints of the Arrow, which were also meant to be destroyed in 1959, were also found in the home of Ken Barnes, a senior draftsman who worked in Avro Canada. The blueprints were then sent to the Diefenbaker Canada Centre in 2020.

In 1997, a miniseries produced by CBC and Heritage Minutes was released, covering the story of the Avro Arrow. The production garnered mixed reactions from the public, especially in reaction to the errors and fictional scenes in the movie. One historian suggested that the movie, at best, evoked a sense of regret and had people thinking about how things could've gone differently hadn't canceled the program. It played on people's imaginations and framed the cancellation as a missed opportunity that prevented Canada from excelling in the global aerospace industry.

The Canada Post also released a commemorative stamp illustrating the Avro Arrow in 2019. This release was part of a stamp issue that honored the technical expertise of all Canadians in the military and civilian aviation industry.

The Avro Arrow was a supersonic, all-whether interceptor that incorporated advanced technologies. It was the first aircraft of its kind to use computer-assisted flight technology and sensors. Everything about the interceptor proved that it was ahead of its time. That said, the creation of the Avro Arrow was brought to a halt due to financial, economic, and political pressures.

Its excellence caused great concern among American aircraft engineers about their inability to compete. The U.S. government was also aware that the Avro Arrow would discover their secret spying mission when the Iroquois engines were installed and tested. The USAF then created the BOMARC missile and pressured the Canadian government to buy it. This, along with the limited defense budget, the lack of international interest in the aircraft, and the limited understanding of new technology, left the Canadian government with no choice but to cancel the program. While the Avro Arrow program ended over 60 years ago, this aircraft's legacy has remained.

Chapter 9: Stories from the October Crisis

The October Crisis brings back memories of a tumultuous and divisive period that tested the very foundations of the Canadian nation. It was a time that shook the nation to its core, sparking a fierce debate over the delicate balance between civil liberties and national security. The late 1960s witnessed the emergence of the Front de libération du Québec (FLQ), a radical separatist group driven by a fervent desire for Quebec's independence from Canada. Their deep-rooted grievances within the province manifested in often violent and uncompromising actions.

The rise of the FLQ, their motivations, and their escalating actions led up to the culmination of events of October 1970. Then came the kidnappings of James Cross and Pierre Laporte, two men whose lives were forever altered by the FLQ's audacious acts. Their abductions marked the point of no return, thrusting Canada into a crisis that would test its resolve and principles.

Central to this chapter is the controversial decision by the federal government to invoke the War Measures Act – an unprecedented move in peacetime Canada. This decision, born out of a desperate desire to restore order and secure the release of the hostages, would ignite passionate debates across the nation. It raised fundamental questions about the trade-off between safeguarding national security and preserving individual freedoms.

41. Rise of the FLQ: Origins and Motivations

The origins and motivations of the Front de libération du Québec (FLQ) are deeply rooted in Quebec's historical, social, and political context during the mid-20th century. The province had long been characterized by a unique cultural identity rooted in its French-speaking population and its Catholic heritage. However, this identity had often been marginalized within the larger Canadian federation. French-speaking Quebecers, known as "Quebecois," faced systemic discrimination, economic inequality, and limited political power.

In the post-World War II era, Quebec began experiencing significant social and economic changes. Urbanization and industrialization transformed the province, leading to increased migration from rural areas to cities like Montreal. This period of rapid change exposed the deep disparities within Quebec society. While some prospered, many working-class Quebecois faced unemployment and poverty.

The 1960s marked the beginning of what is known as the "Quiet Revolution" in Quebec. During this time of tumult, the FLQ began to take shape.

One of the catalysts for the Quiet Revolution was the election of Jean Lesage's Liberal government in 1960. Lesage's administration pursued a progressive agenda to modernize Quebec and address the province's long-standing grievances. Reforms included nationalizing hydroelectric power, improving education, and promoting the French language. These changes ignited a sense of cultural and political awakening among Quebecois, who began to demand greater autonomy and recognition of their distinct identity. However, not all Quebecois agreed on the best path forward. While some advocated for greater autonomy within Canada, others, including the FLQ, believed complete independence was the only solution.

The Front de libération du Québec (FLQ) was founded in 1963, emerging from a milieu of radical and revolutionary ideas that took hold in Quebec during the Quiet Revolution. The FLQ's primary objective was to achieve Quebec's independence from Canada through any means necessary, including armed struggle if required. The FLQ was driven by a fervent sense of Quebecois nationalism. They believed that Quebec was a distinct nation with its own language, culture, and history, and they saw Canadian federalism as an obstacle to fully realizing Quebec's potential.

The FLQ was not averse to using violence to achieve their goals. They believed that armed struggle was a legitimate means of advancing the cause, and this ideology would lead to a series of bombings and violent actions. The FLQ saw the struggle for Quebecois independence as intimately tied to broader social and economic inequality issues and viewed themselves as champions of the working class.

Their ideology also had an anti-imperialist dimension. They saw Canada, especially English-speaking Canada, as a colonial power oppressing Quebec. They drew inspiration from global anti-colonial movements of the time. The FLQ was deeply secular in its outlook. They rejected the influence of the Catholic Church, which had traditionally held significant sway in Quebec, and embraced a more secular and socialist vision for the province.

The FLQ's actions leading up to the October Crisis were fueled by their grievances and frustrations with Quebec's slow pace of political change. One of the earliest incidents of violence was the 1963 bombing of the Montreal Stock Exchange. Over the years, they continued to target symbols of English-Canadian economic power, including banks and government institutions. These acts of terrorism were intended to draw attention to their cause and exert pressure on the government.

The FLQ believed that their violent actions would force the Quebec and Canadian governments to pay attention to their demands for independence. The kidnappings were also aimed at securing the release of FLQ members who had been arrested and imprisoned for previous acts of violence. They hoped that the chaos generated by their actions would create a climate of uncertainty and unrest and saw themselves as revolutionaries who could inspire other marginalized groups, both in Canada and globally, to rise up against perceived oppressors.

42. Pierre Laporte and the October Crisis

By October 1970, Quebec was in the midst of a political and social maelstrom. The FLQ had been escalating its campaign of violence and bombings for several years. Their goal was the complete independence of Quebec from Canada, and they believed that violent actions would force the government's hand. The federal government of Canada, led by Prime Minister Pierre Trudeau, was increasingly concerned about the situation in Quebec. Trudeau, who was himself a Quebecer, was determined to maintain the country's unity.

Pierre Laporte, a prominent figure in Quebec politics, was the Deputy Premier and Minister of Labor in Premier Robert Bourassa's government. He was known for his dedication to public service and commitment to finding peaceful solutions to Quebec's political issues. Unfortunately, this dedication would make him a target for the FLQ. On October 10, 1970, Pierre Laporte's life took a tragic turn. As he played football with his nephew in the front yard of his suburban home in Saint-Lambert, he was abducted by members of the FLQ. This brazen kidnapping sent shockwaves through the nation and raised the stakes of the October Crisis to a new level.

Laporte's captors were determined to use him as a bargaining chip to secure the release of FLQ members imprisoned for their previous acts of terrorism. They issued a list of demands that included the release of 23 imprisoned FLQ members and safe passage to Cuba for themselves. Pierre Laporte's ordeal in captivity was a period of profound uncertainty and fear. He was held in a small, windowless room in a house in Saint-Hubert, a suburb of Montreal. His captors kept him in chains and subjected him to psychological torment, with the constant threat of violence hanging over him.

Laporte's captivity lasted for seven days, during which time he was allowed to write letters to his family. These letters, marked by their heartbreaking desperation, provided glimpses into his state of mind and the harsh conditions of his captivity. He pleaded for his life, begging the authorities to meet the FLQ's demands to secure his release. The kidnapping triggered a massive manhunt and a desperate search to secure his release. The Canadian and Quebec governments were under immense pressure to resolve the crisis. Negotiations were initiated, and intermediaries were brought in to communicate with the FLQ kidnappers.

One of the key figures in these negotiations was Robert Demers, a journalist who had previously reported on the FLQ. Demers became a crucial intermediary between the government and the FLQ, working tirelessly to establish communication and reach a resolution. As days turned into a week, the sense of urgency and tension continued to mount. The nation was on edge, with daily updates on the crisis dominating the news. Public opinion was divided, with some advocating for a peaceful resolution while others urged a more forceful response.

While Pierre Laporte remained in captivity, another dramatic development unfolded. British diplomat James Cross, whom the FLQ had kidnaped on October 5, 1970, was released on December 3, 1970, after being held hostage for 59 days. Cross's release resulted from negotiations that saw some of the FLQ's demands partially met. The release of James Cross marked a significant turning point in the October Crisis. It demonstrated that negotiations could lead to the freedom of hostages, but it also highlighted the FLQ's willingness to resort to violence and kidnapping to advance their cause.

Despite the release of James Cross, the situation remained perilous for Pierre Laporte. Laporte's life took a tragic turn on October 17, 1970, just one day after the federal government enacted the War Measures Act. His captors, fearing a military intervention, decided to escalate the situation. Pierre Laporte was found dead, strangled with a chain, in the trunk of a car abandoned near the Montreal airport. It was a heartbreaking end to the desperate and tragic chapter of the October Crisis. The nation mourned the loss of a dedicated public servant, and the FLQ's actions were met with widespread condemnation.

In the aftermath of the crisis, public sentiment shifted away from the FLQ's tactics of violence and terrorism. The FLQ itself began to lose support among the Quebecois population, as many realized that the group's actions had not advanced the cause of Quebecois independence.

43. The War Measures Act: A Controversial Decision

Prime Minister Pierre Trudeau has to make a difficult decision.
Chiloa, CC BY-SA 3.0 <https://creativecommons.org/licenses/by-sa/3.0>, via Wikimedia Commons: https://commons.wikimedia.org/wiki/File:Pierre_Trudeau.jpg

The decision to invoke the War Measures Act was not made lightly, generating intense debate within the government and among Canadian officials. Prime Minister Pierre Trudeau faced a difficult choice as he grappled with how to respond to the rapidly escalating crisis in Quebec. Some government members believed that a swift and forceful response was necessary to combat the FLQ's violent actions. They argued that the kidnappings and bombings had created a climate of fear and uncertainty. Decisive action was required to restore order and protect Canadian citizens. On the other side, some expressed deep reservations about invoking the War Measures Act. They believed such a move was an overreach of government power and risked infringing upon civil liberties. Critics argued that the FLQ, while a serious threat, did not constitute an armed insurrection or invasion, which were the traditional triggers for the War Measures Act.

On October 16, 1970, Prime Minister Pierre Trudeau announced the decision to invoke the War Measures Act in a televised address to the nation. The government's primary objective was to restore order and ensure the safety of Canadian citizens. The FLQ's actions, including the kidnappings of Pierre Laporte and James Cross, created a crisis and uncertainty in Quebec. The government believed extraordinary measures were needed to bring the situation under control. Officials were genuinely concerned about the FLQ's capabilities and intentions. The group had demonstrated a willingness to use violence, and there were fears that their actions could escalate further. Invoking the War Measures Act was seen as a way to neutralize the FLQ and prevent further violence.

By invoking the War Measures Act, the government wanted to send a strong message that it would not tolerate acts of terrorism and violence. It demonstrated the government's commitment to protecting the integrity of the nation and its citizens. There was also considerable political pressure on the government to take decisive action. Public opinion was divided, with many Canadians demanding a firm response to the crisis. The government's decision reflected a response to these pressures.

The invocation of the Act had a profound impact on civil liberties. It granted the government extensive powers, including the ability to arrest and detain individuals without a warrant and to conduct searches without consent. These measures were seen as necessary to combat the FLQ threat, but they raised serious concerns about civil liberties. Under the authority of the Act, over 450 people were arrested and detained without charge. These individuals were held without the standard legal safeguards and protections usually afforded to Canadian citizens, leading to accusations of arbitrary and unjust imprisonment.

The suspension of habeas corpus, a fundamental legal principle that safeguards against arbitrary detention, was a contentious aspect of the War Measures Act. It meant individuals could be held without the right to challenge their detention in court. The Act also allowed for media censorship, with the government having the power to control and limit information disseminated to the public. This raised concerns about freedom of the press and the right to access information.

The imposition of the War Measures Act disproportionately affected the Quebecois population, as most of the FLQ's activities were centered in Quebec. Many Quebecois felt they were being unfairly targeted and that their civil liberties were being violated. The use of the War Measures Act during the October Crisis had long-term consequences for civil liberties in Canada. It raised questions about the balance between national security and individual rights, leading to increased scrutiny of government actions in times of crisis.

44. Voices of the Public: Reactions and Responses

For many Canadians, the October Crisis was a time of fear and anxiety. The sudden and shocking kidnappings of Pierre Laporte and James Cross sent shockwaves throughout the country. People worried about their safety and the safety of their loved ones. The government's decision to invoke the War Measures Act was met with mixed opinions. Some Canadians supported the move, viewing it as necessary to quell the violence and restore order. They saw it as a demonstration of the government's commitment to protecting its citizens. However, others were deeply critical, expressing concerns about civil liberties and the potential for government overreach. Interviews with citizens reveal the depth of these divisions within the Canadian public.

The October Crisis prompted a nationwide debate about the balance between national security and individual rights. In letters to the editor, radio call-in shows, and community meetings, Canadians engaged in spirited discussions about the government's actions. Some argued passionately for a strong response to the FLQ threat, while others advocated for a more measured approach. These conversations reflected the deeply held beliefs and values of the Canadian public. While the crisis was centered in Quebec, Canadians from other provinces also had a significant stake in its resolution. Many expressed solidarity with the Quebecois people, recognizing their grievances and desire for greater autonomy. This sentiment was particularly evident in messages of support and empathy sent to Quebec from across the country. Canadians sought to bridge the regional divide and build understanding during this trying time.

The release of James Cross and the tragic death of Pierre Laporte evoked contrasting emotions. Canadians were relieved when Cross was freed after nearly two months in captivity. It was a moment of jubilation and hope as people celebrated the safe return of a fellow citizen. However, the discovery of Laporte's lifeless body in a car trunk near the Montreal airport casts a pall of mourning and sorrow over the nation. Public expressions of condolences and tributes poured in, highlighting the human toll of the crisis.

45. The FLQ and Its Legacy

The Front de libération du Québec left a lasting legacy on Quebecois nationalism and separatism, with their actions reverberating through the province's politics and having a long-term impact on the Quebec sovereignty movement. The FLQ's actions during the 1960s and the October Crisis of 1970 served to heighten Quebecois nationalism. While not all Quebecois supported their violent methods, the FLQ tapped into a deep-seated sentiment that Quebec's unique cultural and linguistic identity deserved greater recognition and autonomy. The crisis spotlighted the perceived injustices faced by Quebecois, leading to increased calls for linguistic and cultural preservation. The FLQ's radicalism and violence also polarized Quebecois society. While some saw them as champions of Quebec's cause, others viewed them as extremists who tarnished the province's image. This polarization within Quebecois society contributed to a sense of division that would persist in Quebec politics for decades.

In the aftermath of the October Crisis, the Quebec government, led by Premier Robert Bourassa, implemented measures to address the root causes of separatist sentiment. These included policies to promote the French language and Quebecois culture. The FLQ's actions indirectly influenced the direction of Quebec politics, pushing the province towards a more assertive stance within the Canadian Federation. Perhaps one of the most significant legacies of the FLQ was the rise of the Parti Québécois (PQ). Founded in 1968, the PQ was a political party committed to achieving Quebecois independence through democratic means. The FLQ's actions contributed to the PQ's electoral success, as many Quebecois turned away from violent separatism in favor of a political route to sovereignty.

The lasting influence of the FLQ was evident in the 1980 and 1995 referendums on Quebec sovereignty. While neither referendum resulted in Quebec's secession from Canada, they showcased the enduring longevity of Quebecois nationalism and the FLQ's role in shaping the political landscape. The "Quiet Revolution" that had begun in the 1960s continued, with Quebec asserting its cultural and linguistic identity within Canada.

The use of the War Measures Act raised unanswered questions about the balance between national security and civil liberties. The crisis underscored the need for clear guidelines and safeguards during states of emergency, leading to ongoing debates over the powers of government in times of crisis.

The October Crisis had a profound impact on Canadian politics. It influenced discussions about Quebec's role within Canada, the protection of minority rights, and the relationship between the federal government and provinces. The crisis served as a catalyst for constitutional negotiations and discussions about the Canadian Constitution's repatriation, culminating in the Canada Act of 1982.

The October Crisis remains a defining moment in modern Canadian history. It continues to be studied in classrooms, analyzed in political discourse, and referenced in discussions about the relationship between individual rights and national security. The crisis serves as a reminder of Canadian federalism's complex and sometimes contentious nature and the ongoing pursuit of a just balance between unity and diversity.

Chapter 10: Tales of Human Rights and Freedoms in Canada

Starting with the story of the Canadian Charter of Rights and Freedom, this final chapter gives an insight into how human rights and legislative change have evolved over the country's history. After learning about the early foundations of human rights, the chapter segues into significant moments, like the tale of the Persons Case, a major turning point in women's rights in Canada. After these notable legal cases that tested and shaped people's rights and freedoms, you'll read a story of how the Truth and Reconciliation Commission set on a journey toward acknowledging Indigenous rights, challenges, and justice through their dynamic and evolving nature. The stories of Tommy Douglas, the father of Medicare, and Chief Justice Beverley McLachlin will provide an even more profound insight into how far Canada has come as a nation in many aspects of human rights.

46. The Canadian Charter of Rights and Freedoms: A Milestone in Nationhood

The Canadian Charter of Rights and Freedoms.

Canadian Heritage, OGL-C 2.0 <http://open.canada.ca/en/open-government-licence-canada>, via Wikimedia Commons:

https://commons.wikimedia.org/wiki/File:Canadian_Charter_of_Rights_and_Freedoms_(English).jpg

A fundamental element of Canada's Constitution signed in 1982, the Canadian Charter of Rights and Freedoms drastically shaped the evolution of human rights. Over time, it changed how freedom is viewed and protected nationwide. Following the age-old British legal tradition, before 1982, the Parliament was in charge of the human rights laws. However, this meant the legislative department had a supreme rule – and if it wanted to change any law, it could easily do so by influencing the parliament's judicial branch. In other words, laws did not guarantee human rights, as these could be changed at will. Even if one parliament passed a law, the next could modify or strike it.

The Canadian Bill of Rights was passed as a halfhearted attempt to protect human rights in 1960. However, due to parliamentary supremacy, the Parliament could still modify it. Moreover, if the legislative branch found it fit to use other laws to override the Bill of Rights, it could also do it. This rendered any bill ineffective in many cases, especially when protecting human rights and freedom. The solution to this issue was simple, although slow in the making. Canada needed a bill governing and protecting human rights that could be incorporated into the Constitution.

By contrast, the Canadian Charter of Rights and Freedoms, enacted in 1982, granted essential rights and freedoms now protected by Canada's Constitution. It banned discrimination based on age, sex, color, disability, and religion, established Indigenous and treaty, and affirmed language-based rights.

While undoubtedly a monumental milestone, the Charter still left plenty of room for interpretation. For example, some interpreted it in a way that allowed the protection of Indigenous status. Others have applied it to fight against discrimination based on marital status or sexual orientation but haven't seen it as protection on any other basis.

An equally significant aspect was that it gave the full authority of the country's highest law to Canada. The much debated and criticized separation from the British legislature had people in fear of possible unilateral actions of the federal government. Due to these fears and opposition, the Charter was written up and enacted without Quebec's approval.

Still, as part of the Canadian Constitution, the Charter became the country's supreme law. To this day, no other law can overrule the rights it shields. Moreover, the Canadian court has the authority to nullify any legislature that goes against the Charter or any other constitutional principle. In court cases, judges can strike any law that violates human rights and freedom, granting the latter automatically.

47. The Persons Case: A Turning Point for Women's Rights

Except for Quebec, most provinces granted women voting rights by 1927. At first, Canadian women over the age of 21 only could have a say in federal elections. They did, however, later acquire the ability to run in the House of Commons for office. Agnes Macphail, the first female member of the organization, joined in 1921. However, Canadian women were still denied entrance to the Senate due to a provision of the 1867 Constitution Act. This document proclaimed that only certain "persons" could become Senate members. To determine whether they qualified, individuals only had to meet a few criteria, none of which referred to the "person's" gender. However, at the time, the default legal definition of the term "persons" was male. Consequently, the Constitution Acts section in question implied only men could join the Senate.

In a ground-breaking initiative supported by the National Council of Women of Canada, the Federated Women's Institutes, and the Montreal Women's Club, Alberta activists brought up the issue of Emily Murphy, Canada's first female judge, joining the Senate. Despite being celebrated by the champion of women in the judicial system, the government dismissed Murphy's admittance to the Senate, referencing the 1867 Constitution Act's definition of a "person." Not that Murphy wasn't expecting this. Like many other new female members of the Canadian judicial system, she was often dismissed as a lawyer and judge for being a woman.

Five other governments played with the idea of having female Senate members in the years that followed. However, the Constitution Act still rendered this impossible. In 1923, there were talks about a proposition to amend the act, but this never materialized. In 1927, Emily Murphy had enough of the government's stalling efforts and constant referral to the limiting legal document. Murphy teamed together with women's rights campaigners Irene Parlby, Henrietta Muir Edwards, Louise McKinney, and Nellie McClung to request the Supreme Court to interpret a legal issue in the Constitution Act under Section 60 of the Supreme Court Act. The five women signed a petition addressed to the governor-general asking the Supreme Court to rule on the constitutionality of the Canadian Parliament's ability to provide for female Senate members, whether that reference is made to the Constitution Act or not, and whether the Parliament of Canada or the Governor-General in Council of Canada has the authority to decide whether women may be admitted to the Senate. The Canadian minister of justice during that time thought it was unheard of for women to even get a Supreme Court decision on anything. The Supreme Court, however, took its time debating whether women were included in the term "person" in the notorious part of the British North America Act. Sadly, their response was unfavorable. As a result, women could not serve in the Senate in 1928 because they were still not considered "persons" under Canadian law. Two arguments buttressed the decision. One simply claimed that if the act had intended to welcome women into the Senate, it would have specified this. The second one premised that (despite the numerous changes in the Canadian judicial system), the act in question must be interpreted the same way it was accepted in 1867.

Still, the five women (the Famous Five as they became known through their fight) were not deterred. They requested a review of the Supreme Court's ruling from the Judicial Committee of the Privy Council in London, Canada's highest court of appeal at the time. The verdict was much more positive this time. The Privy Council overturned the Supreme Court's decision and determined that women are included in the phrase "persons" in Section 24. As of right now, women could be appointed to Canada's Senate. They could now advocate for changes in both the House of Commons and the Senate. However, the final results of the case (entered as the Persons Case into history books) had a much more profound impact on women's rights in Canada. The victory meant that their rights must be upheld regardless of the interpretation of the law.

Women obtained the right to run for provincial office in March 1934 in most provinces, except in Quebec, where this liberty was granted to them in 1940. However, non-White women faced further difficulties when it came to obtaining voting rights. For example, the Métis women could only vote if they met specific qualifications, like property ownership and being of a certain age. Inuit women were granted voting rights in 1950, while the First Nations women only obtained this in 1960.

The Famous Five have been the subject of harsh criticism. While female activities were viewed as harbingers of progress and signs of much-needed modernization, others argued they were elitists and racists. They were associated with legislatures that enacted the forced sterilization of (mainly) indigenous women and other facets of the infamous eugenics movement.

Still, the significance of the group's achievement can't be denied or diminished. Cairine Wilson became Canada's first female senator as a result of their triumph in the early 1930s. Wilson's appointment had other far-reaching effects in addition to reaffirming the notion that women were now viewed as "persons" by the law. This was a pivotal occasion in the history of women's rights, along with the Persons Case in general. However, the fight for equality for women, almost a century later, is still going strong.

In 1979, the Governor General's Awards were established to keep the legacy of the Persons Case alive. Each year, the recipients are five people who make significant contributions to improving women's rights in Canada. A memorial with the slogan "Women are Persons!" was built in Calgary's Olympic Plaza in 1999. After that, Ottawa's Parliament Hill had a similar monument put up. The Royal Canadian Mint's Canadian Journey Series $50 banknote features an illustration of the latter.

48. Truth and Reconciliation: The Journey Towards Indigenous Rights and Justice

As part of the Indian Residential Schools Settlement Agreement, The Truth and Reconciliation Commission (TRC) was put together in 2007 to gather information about the consequences of the Indian Residential Schools system. Besides granting the floor to former students, their families, and communities to speak about their experiences, it also ensured the rest of the non-Indigenous population would listen and learn about these truths. The goal was to foster reconciliation between all Canadians.

For six years, members of the Commission journeyed across the country, collecting testimonies of the Inuit, Métis, and First Nation community members and leaders. They also organized several events, prompting the Canadian public to educate themselves about how the residential school systems worked and how they affected Indigenous communities. The testimonies collected from former students and their communities also created a detailed analysis of the system. The record of this analysis found a permanent home at The National Centre for Truth and Reconciliation at the University of Manitoba.

In 2015, The National Centre for Truth and Reconciliation created a final report, including findings and recommendations on encouraging further reconciliation between the Indigenous and non-Indigenous communities. Accepted on behalf of the Canadian government by Prime Minister Justin Trudeau, this final report begins by giving homage to the courage of each former student and their community members who shared their views of the heartbreaking legacy of the residential schools. As a result, the governments became even more committed to rebuilding the relationships between the different nations, encouraging cooperation, mutual respect, and acknowledging Indigenous rights. It continues to seek recommendations from the TRC and the representatives of Métis,

First Nation, and Inuit people on how to speed up reconciliation. As the first step towards this goal, the Canadian government adopted the United Nations Declaration on the Rights of Indigenous Peoples, reversing its previous decision of voting against it.

By working in partnership with Indigenous communities affected by the residential schools and following the TRC recommendations, the government set several goals toward reconciliation. These include acknowledging past injustices and finding ways to heal, encouraging advancement in prosperity and self-determination, and fostering strong communities with healthy relationships within and outward.

As part of the system for addressing past injustices and healing, the TRC recommended focusing on specific claims and conceiving an action plan on how to approach these to improve inter-community relationships.

When working with Métis, Inuit, and First Nations members, the focus was put on providing better access to essential services, including safe housing, clean drinking water, emergency, physical and mental health care, natural resources, and encouraging self-determination to seek improvement for individuals and communities and resources to address the effects of climate change. All these will go a long way toward building and maintaining a powerful relationship based on recognition and respect for rights. The adoption of the UN Declaration on the Rights of Indigenous Peoples Act also means that Indigenous communities now enjoy greater protection of their language, treaties, and other agreements and can seek education more freely. This prompted a step toward economic reconciliation with non-indigenous communities, another enormous milestone in the human rights revolution in Canada.

49. Tommy Douglas: The Father of Medicare

Tommy Douglas made a well-organized healthcare system possible.
https://commons.wikimedia.org/wiki/File:Tommy_Douglas_1955.jpg

Canada is the proud owner of one of the world's most well-organized healthcare systems, and it was all made possible by Tommy Douglas, the former Premier of the Saskatchewan province. At first, he promised policies that would change many aspects of the social system, inducing human rights and healthcare. Due to their numerous benefits, including improving quality of life and fighting against social injustice, the policies were soon implemented nationally, too.

Nowadays, Medicare makes Canada one of the best countries in terms of healthcare access. However, this wasn't always the case. During the 1930s Great Depression era, the entire continent lacked access to medical care. Being one of the most neglected Canadian provinces at the time, Saskatchewan also fell victim to poor infrastructure, resulting in unsafe conditions for public health care workers and patients alike. Not that they even tried to seek medical care. Without mandated minimum wages or a workers' union that would fight for these, people often did not have enough money to seek medical help. With inadequate public healthcare organizations, only those who could afford private services could save themselves from the troubles brought on by physical or mental disabilities, accidents, and illnesses.

Needless to say, Tommy Douglas's decision to implement a publicly funded hospital insurance plan in Saskatchewan in 1947 was a much-welcome change. A year later, Ontario, British Columbia, and Alberta also adopted similar policies, and soon, the federal government started providing grants to fund these plans in each province.

A few years after the Hospital Insurance and Diagnostic Services Act was enacted. In 1957, the remaining Canadian provinces also signed up for the universal hospital care coverage system. The last step was the enactment of the Canada Health Act in 1984 – another significant milestone on this journey toward better healthcare started by Tommy Douglas. This legislation issued by the Canadian government defines the criteria and conditions public health insurance programs across the country work by to obtain funds. While the individual provinces are free to choose whether to adhere to this act, most find the financial benefits an excellent incentive to do so. Due to this, the health of all Canadians can be maintained and improved without financial limitations. Everyone can have access to quality healthcare and have their physical and mental well-being restored, improved, and rights protected.

Tommy Douglas, now known as the father of this much-improved public healthcare system, greatly influenced how Canada deals with healthcare even today. It took much determination and hard work for him to face those opposed to his ideas, which were many. However, he stood by his convictions and showed the entire country that if there was a need for a system that would improve the lives of many, there was also a solution to build it. As the champion of all those who couldn't afford private health care, Tommy Douglas helped improve people's quality of life in his and all generations that followed.

Besides ensuring immediate access to medical care, he laid the groundwork for healthcare and insurance policies for the elderly, the disabled or marginalized, workers, and every other citizen in the country.

50. Chief Justice Beverley McLachlin – The First Female Chief Justice of the Canadian Supreme Court

Born and raised in an isolated farming community in Pincher Creek, Alberta, Beverley McLachlin learned the powers of perseverance and community early on. After earning a Bachelor of Arts in Philosophy in 1965, she started pursuing a degree in law at her soon-to-be husband's suggestion. Staying true to her hard-working nature, she worked on her Master of Art in Philosophy and Bachelor of Law, both of which she gained in 1968. After a rocky start to secure the mandatory clerkship (law firms weren't keen on employing women, much less married women, at the time), she was admitted to the Alberta Bar in 1969. To find better practice opportunities, she moved to British Columbia in 1971 and was called to the Bar here as well. She also had the chance to nurse her passion for academia since her formative years while acting as a tenured Associate Professor in the Faculty of Law at the University of British Columbia from 1974 to 1981.

In the spring of 1981, Beverley McLachlin started her long and prosperous judicial career when she was appointed first as a judge at the Vancouver County Court after Prime Minister Pierre Trudeau raised the question of the lack of female representation in the federal judiciary. Half a year later, she became a superior court trial judge at the Supreme Court of British Columbia. After being elevated to the Chief Justice of the Supreme Court of British Columbia position in 1989, and as Justice of the Supreme Court of Canada in 1989, she obtained the title that would forever etch her name into the history books – she was sworn in as the first female Chief Justice of Canada. Besides fulfilling her duties at the Supreme Court and publishing numerous articles and books, Chief Justice Beverley McLachlin was also the chairwoman of the Advisory Council of the Order of Canada, the Board of Governors of the National Judicial Institute, and the Advisory Council of the Order of Canada until her retirement in 2017.

Conclusion

At the beginning of your journey across Canada's history, you were introduced to the Inuit and Métis people. By exploring their ancestral roots, cultural traditions, and spiritual beliefs, you had a chance to see how their roles shaped Canada. Despite having to contend with Canada's challenging environments and shaky interactions with European settlers, the rich tapestry of their cultural and societal structure allowed them to adapt to circumstances. The perspective of Indigenous societies even impacted French explorer Jaques Cartier's journey across Canada. Led by the European need for exploration and the desire for new trade routes, Cartier's voyage and subsequent claim of Canada for France and mapping the St. Lawrence River had extraordinary significance for Canada's future.

Next, you met the Huron-Wendat people and learned about their society and culture through stories about their history. The strategic use of fur during this era fueled numerous conflicts, including the Beaver Wars. Besides the undeniable environmental impact, these battles had long-term effects on the Huron-Wendat and other tribes and the formation of Canada.

The next chapter explored the roots of French-Canadian identity, factoring in their unique cultural heritage, language, and religion. The subsequent chapter introduced stories about the Canadian Confederation, touching on subjects like the political climate and motivations that spurred the push for this event (like the Charlottetown Conference) and the immediate and long-term implications of Confederation on Canada's development as a nation.

As you learned from the dedicated chapter, despite the discovery of gold, the rush of prospectors, and the rapid growth of Dawson City (and later the economy and infrastructure of Yukon and Canada), the Klondike journey contained much harsher surprises – especially for the Indigenous people. However, during World War I, the entire country learned the meaning of sacrifice while facing the toll of war with courage and determination.

Through the Avro Arrow Saga stories, you've read of the significance of this ambitious aerospace project. Besides introducing the Avro Arrow, its intended role, and its advanced technological features, the chapter details the project's development, emphasizing the dedication and skills of Canadian engineers – along with the circumstances leading to its controversial cancellation and the loss of skilled soldiers.

The penultimate chapter deals with even more somber facets of Canadian history – the October Crisis. Reading it, you had the chance to see what led to the rise of the Front de libération du Québec, events like the kidnappings of James Cross and Pierre Laporte, and the federal government's unprecedented invocation of the War Measures Act. To conclude your journey, you've gained an insight into the colorful evolution of human rights and Canadian legislative change over the last few years. From the early foundations of human rights through the introduction of the Canadian Bill of Rights and the subsequent adoption of the Canadian Charter of Rights and Freedoms, the process had many ups and downs. Yet, it all shows how far Canada has come as a nation.

Check out another book in the series

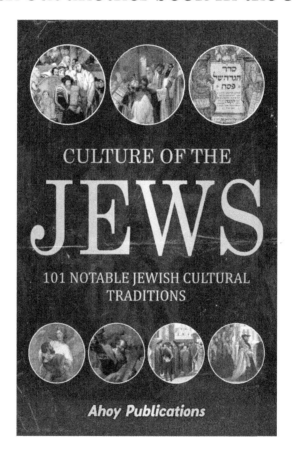

References

(N.d.). Historyofrights.Ca. https://historyofrights.ca/wp-content/uploads/documents/FLQ_appendixz.pdf

(N.d.). Umaine.edu. https://umaine.edu/teachingcanada/wp-content/uploads/sites/176/2015/06/Henri-Bourassa-Levitt.pdf

Allaire, B. (n.d.). Jacques Cartier. Thecanadianencyclopedia.Ca. https://www.thecanadianencyclopedia.ca/en/article/jacques-cartier

An Introduction to Canadian History. (2015, October 15). Humber College. https://humber.ca/course/introduction-canadian-history

An Introduction to Canadian History. (n.d.). Queensu.Ca. https://www.queensu.ca/artsci_online/courses/an-introduction-to-canadian-history

Arseneau, J. (2017, November 16). Canada's failed revolution: the rebellions of 1837-1838. In Defence of Marxism. https://www.marxist.com/canada-s-failed-revolution-the-rebellions-of-1837-1838.htm

Avro Arrow. (n.d.-a). The Canadian Encyclopedia. https://www.thecanadianencyclopedia.ca/en/article/avro-arrow

Avro Arrow. (n.d.-b). Canadian Science & Technology Museum Corporation. https://ingeniumcanada.org/channel/innovation/avro-arrow

Battle of passchendaele. (n.d.). Nam.ac.uk. https://www.nam.ac.uk/explore/battle-passchendaele

Battle of Quebec 1775: Date & American Revolution. (2009, November 2). HISTORY. https://www.history.com/topics/american-revolution/battle-of-quebec-1775

Battle of Quebec. (n.d.). Nam.ac.uk. https://www.nam.ac.uk/explore/battle-quebec

Belshaw, J. D. (2015). 1.1 introduction. In Canadian History: Pre-Confederation. BCcampus.

Belshaw, J. D. (2015). 1.1 introduction. In Canadian History: Pre-Confederation. BCcampus.

Borden, S. R. (n.d.). Life at home during the war – the home front. Canada and the First World War. https://www.warmuseum.ca/firstworldwar/history/life-at-home-during-the-war/the-home-front/

Buckner, P. A. (n.d.). Rebellion in Lower Canada (the patriots' war). Thecanadianencyclopedia.Ca. https://www.thecanadianencyclopedia.ca/en/article/rebellion-in-lower-canada

Canada A Country by Consent: Newfoundland Joins Canada. (n.d.). Canadahistoryproject.Ca. https://canadahistoryproject.ca/1949/index.html

Canada, V. A. (2019, August 8). Canada remembers women on the home front. Veterans.Gc.Ca. https://www.veterans.gc.ca/eng/remembrance/those-who-served/women-veterans/homefront

Canada, V. A. (2020, January 23). First world war (1914 – 1918) – veterans affairs Canada. Veterans.Gc.Ca. https://www.veterans.gc.ca/eng/remembrance/wars-and-conflicts/first-world-war/

Canada, V. A. (2022, July 12). Battle of Vimy Ridge. Veterans.Gc.Ca. https://www.veterans.gc.ca/eng/remembrance/wars-and-conflicts/first-world-war/battle-of-vimy-ridge

Canada's Jet-Age Dream: The Avro Arrow – Google Arts & Culture. (n.d.). Google Arts & Culture. https://artsandculture.google.com/story/canada%E2%80%99s-jet-age-dream-the-avro-arrow-canada-aviation-and-space-museum/RgWh1ZCGfwg4IQ?hl=en

Canada's Role in WWI. (n.d.). Mta.Ca. https://www.mta.ca/library/courage/canadasroleinwwi.html

Canadian Geographic. (2018, June 5). Red River Resistance. Indigenouspeoplesatlasofcanada.Ca; Canadian Geographic. https://indigenouspeoplesatlasofcanada.ca/article/red-river-resistance/

Canadian History/Introduction. (n.d.). Wikibooks.Org. https://en.wikibooks.org/wiki/Canadian_History/Introduction

Canadian Museum of History. (n.d.). Stories of Confederation. Teachers' Zone | Canadian Museum of History. https://www.historymuseum.ca/teachers-zone/stories-of-confederation/

Carmack), S. T. (kate. (n.d.). Keish (Skookum Jim Mason) (U.s. national Park service). Nps.gov. https://www.nps.gov/people/keish-skookum-jim.htm

Cartier, W. by J. (n.d.). Jacques Cartier. Newworldencyclopedia.org. https://www.newworldencyclopedia.org/entry/Jacques_Cartier

Chilkoot pass: The "golden staircase." (n.d.). Washington.edu.
https://www.lib.washington.edu/specialcollections/collections/exhibits/klondike/case7-8

Chilkoot Trail history – Klondike Gold Rush National Historical Park (U.S. National Park service). (n.d.). Nps.gov.
https://www.nps.gov/klgo/learn/historyculture/chilkoot-history.htm

Civilization.Ca – history of Canadian Medicare – 1958-1968 – autonomy in La Belle province. (n.d.). Historymuseum.Ca.

Confederation (plain-language summary). (n.d.). Thecanadianencyclopedia.Ca.
https://www.thecanadianencyclopedia.ca/en/article/confederation-plain-language-summary

Curtis, A. (2021, August 3). Avro Arrow | VALOUR CANADA. VALOUR CANADA. https://valourcanada.ca/military-history-library/avro-arrow/

Empire of the Bay: Jacques Cartier. (n.d.). Pbs.org.
https://www.pbs.org/empireofthebay/profiles/cartier.html

Erb, M. C. (2020, August 14). Justice Beverley McLachlin: A Remarkable Journey to the 'Centre Chair.' Judicature | The Scholarly Journal About the Judiciary. https://judicature.duke.edu/articles/a-remarkable-journey-to-the-centre-chair/

Fidler, R. (n.d.). Remembering Québec's October crisis. Canadiandimension.com.
https://canadiandimension.com/articles/view/remembering-quebecs-october-crisis

Fidler, R. (n.d.). Remembering Québec's October crisis. Canadiandimension.com.
https://canadiandimension.com/articles/view/remembering-quebecs-october-crisis

Foot, R., & Bumsted, J. M. (2016). Red River Rebellion. In Encyclopedia Britannica.

French Canada's new voice. (n.d.). CBC News.
https://www.cbc.ca/history/EPISCONTENTSE1EP11CH2PA4LE.html

Geloso, V., & Kufenko, V. (2018). Markets for rebellions? The rebellions of 1837-38 in lower Canada. SSRN Electronic Journal.
https://doi.org/10.2139/ssrn.3235561

Government of Canada, Relations, C.-I., & Northern Affairs Canada. (2015, December 14). Truth and Reconciliation Commission of Canada. Rcaanc-Cirnac.Gc.Ca. https://www.rcaanc-cirnac.gc.ca/eng/1450124405592/1529106060525

Government of Canada, Relations, C.-I., & Northern Affairs Canada. (2022, May 6). The reconciliation journey. Rcaanc-Cirnac.Gc.Ca. https://www.rcaanc-cirnac.gc.ca/eng/1651868378940/1651868435684

Guo, S. Z. (2020, November 3). Avro Arrow: An Untimely Legend – Simon Zirui Guo – Medium. Medium. https://simonguozirui.medium.com/avro-arrow-an-untimely-legend-a0e9ca7d4a14

Hand, T. (2023, June 15). Americana Corner: The Iroquois Confederacy. Local Columnist. https://www.bryancountynews.com/opinion/americana-corner-iroquois-confederacy/

Historic Background. (2022, July 31). Sainte-Marie among the Hurons. https://saintemarieamongthehurons.on.ca/about-us/historic-background/

History of the White Pass trail – Klondike Gold Rush National Historical Park (U.S. National Park service). (n.d.). Nps.gov. https://www.nps.gov/klgo/learn/historyculture/white-pass-history.htm

History of Vimy Ridge. (n.d.). Vimyfoundation.Ca. https://vimyfoundation.ca/learn/vimy-ridge

Introduction to Canadian History. (n.d.). Mr. Caners' Class: 2016-2017. http://mrcaners.weebly.com/introduction-to-canadian-history.html

Jacques Cartier – ages of exploration. (2013, November 16). Marinersmuseum.org. https://exploration.marinersmuseum.org/subject/jacques-cartier/

Jacques Cartier. (2009, November 9). HISTORY. https://www.history.com/topics/exploration/jacques-cartier

Jones, R. (n.d.). French Canadian nationalism. Thecanadianencyclopedia.Ca. https://www.thecanadianencyclopedia.ca/en/article/french-canadian-nationalism

Klondike Gold Rush. (2018, January 17). HISTORY. https://www.history.com/topics/19th-century/klondike-gold-rush

Klondike gold rush. (n.d.). Dawson City Yukon. https://dawsoncity.ca/discover-dawson/klondike-gold-rush/

Log Cabin metropolis: Circle City – Yukon – Charley Rivers National Preserve (U.S. National Park Service). (n.d.). Nps.gov. https://www.nps.gov/yuch/learn/historyculture/circle-city.htm

Mason, James "Skookum" Jim (Kèsh) National Historic Person. (n.d.). https://www.pc.gc.ca/apps/dfhd/page_nhs_eng.aspx?id=1703

Mathew, R. (n.d.). Expert-Eyes: the Great Whale Project. Expert-Eyes.Org. https://www.expert-eyes.org/whale.html

McIntosh, A., & Cooper, C. (n.d.). October Crisis. Thecanadianencyclopedia.Ca. https://www.thecanadianencyclopedia.ca/en/article/october-crisis

McIntosh, A., & Cooper, C. (n.d.). October Crisis. Thecanadianencyclopedia.Ca. https://www.thecanadianencyclopedia.ca/en/article/october-crisis

McIntosh, A., Waite, P. B., & Martin, G. (n.d.). Charlottetown Conference. Thecanadianencyclopedia.Ca. https://www.thecanadianencyclopedia.ca/en/article/charlottetown-conference

Monique D. Auger, M. S. (2021). Understanding our past, reclaiming our culture: Métis resistance, resilience, and connection to land in the face of colonialism. Journal of Indigenous, 10(1).

Munroe, S. (2005, April 21). What was the Canadian Confederation? ThoughtCo. https://www.thoughtco.com/confederation-510087

Newfoundland. (n.d.). Cambridge.org. https://dictionary.cambridge.org/us/dictionary/english/newfoundland

Palframan, J. R. (n.d.). Lifting the veil of violence: The October crisis. Kennesaw.edu. https://digitalcommons.kennesaw.edu/cgi/viewcontent.cgi?article=1014&context=ojur

Perla, A. (n.d.). The Canadian Charter of Rights and Freedoms. CMHR. https://humanrights.ca/story/canadian-charter-rights-and-freedoms

Persons Case. (n.d.). Thecanadianencyclopedia.Ca. https://www.thecanadianencyclopedia.ca/en/article/persons-case

Red River Resistance. (n.d.). Thecanadianencyclopedia.Ca. https://www.thecanadianencyclopedia.ca/en/article/red-river-rebellion

Robinson, A. (n.d.). Manifest Destiny. Thecanadianencyclopedia.Ca. https://thecanadianencyclopedia.ca/en/article/manifest-destiny

Supreme Court of Canada. (2001, January 1). Supreme Court of Canada – Biography – Beverley McLachlin. Scc-Csc.Ca. https://www.scc-csc.ca/judges-juges/bio-eng.aspx?id=beverley-mclachlin

taniam. (2022, May 10). 1640 – 1701 – Beaver Wars (French and Iroquois Wars) Force Relocation to Door County, Wisconsin. NHBP. https://nhbp-nsn.gov/timeline/1640-1701/

Tattrie, J., & McIntosh, A. (n.d.). Newfoundland and Labrador and Confederation. Thecanadianencyclopedia.Ca. https://www.thecanadianencyclopedia.ca/en/article/newfoundland-and-labrador-and-confederation

The Battle of Quebec. (n.d.). Theamericanrevolution.org. http://theamericanrevolution.org/battledetail.aspx?battle=6

The battle of Vimy Ridge. (n.d.). Warmuseum.Ca. https://www.warmuseum.ca/the-battle-of-vimy-ridge/

The Canadian Encyclopedia. (n.d.). Quiet Revolution (plain-language summary). Thecanadianencyclopedia.Ca. https://www.thecanadianencyclopedia.ca/en/article/quiet-revolution-plain-language-summary

The Canadian Encyclopedia. (n.d.). Sir John A. Macdonald. Thecanadianencyclopedia.Ca. https://www.thecanadianencyclopedia.ca/en/article/sir-john-alexander-macdonald

The Huron-Wendat in Wendake. (2017, June 7). The Story of Ste. Marie II. https://www.communitystories.ca/v2/story-of_histoire-de-ste-marie-n/story/huron-wendat-wendake/

The October Crisis. (n.d.). CBC News. https://www.cbc.ca/history/EPISCONTENTSE1EP16CH1PA4LE.html

The October Crisis. (n.d.). CBC News. https://www.cbc.ca/history/EPISCONTENTSE1EP16CH1PA4LE.html

The search for remnants of the Avro Arrow in Lake Ontario concludes with a discovery. (n.d.). Global News. https://globalnews.ca/video/7358157/the-search-for-remnants-of-the-avro-arrow-in-lake-ontario-concludes-with-a-discovery

Tommy Douglas: Father of Medicare and the Canadian Universal Healthcare System. (n.d.). Linkedin.Com. https://www.linkedin.com/pulse/tommy-douglas-father-medicare-canadian-universal-som-mbbs-mba/

Verhovek, S. H. (1992, January 12). Power Struggle. The New York Times. https://www.nytimes.com/1992/01/12/magazine/power-struggle.html

Waite, P. B. (n.d.). Confederation. Thecanadianencyclopedia.Ca. https://www.thecanadianencyclopedia.ca/en/article/confederation

Wendat (Huron). (n.d.). Thecanadianencyclopedia.Ca. https://www.thecanadianencyclopedia.ca/en/article/huron

What you need to know about the Third Battle of Ypres. (n.d.). Imperial War Museums. https://www.iwm.org.uk/history/what-you-need-to-know-about-the-third-battle-of-ypres-passchendaele

Yu, C. (n.d.). Quebec History. http://faculty.marianopolis.edu/c.belanger/quebechistory/federal/johna.htm

Printed in Great Britain
by Amazon

40454921R00066